Unraveling The Weave

By

Ellen Marie Blend

Unraveling The Weave

A LeasCon Book: Image Ink Publications
                   LeasCon Corporation
                   46882 Jans Drive
                   New Baltimore, MI 48047

Copy edited by Pamela M. Green
Assistant Editor Toni Rodgers

Library of Congress Number: 2001086107
ISBN: 1-929219-02-4
First printing: October 2001

Copies of this book may be obtained through major bookstores,
wholesalers and distributors or by visiting Ellen Blend's Web Site:

http://www.ellenblend.com

The editor may be contacted at:

editor@ellenblend.com

Dedication

This book is dedicated to all those who found pleasure in reading "Visual Encounters" and those who share my intrigue with the spiritual world. While some license has been taken to assign ownership of restless family spirits to current family members as well as to still-to-be-found tombstones of a faraway land, it is that "leap of faith" that provides satisfying answers to unsolved mysteries. In regard to my friends and family members of whom I write, I particularly dedicate this book to you.

Watch for These Titles Coming Soon

Author:
Ellen Marie Blend

Looking Back

Conversing on a Higher Level

Real Objectivity

When Is It My Turn?

Also Written by this Author

Visual Encounters

Contents

Introduction

For years I had seen what I called "visions" in my mind's eye. They were symbolic images in regard to a person that represented something about their life. I saw beyond the person's physical being. It somehow looked more inward, to their internal self, maybe even their very soul.

The seeing of these visions developed from having no understanding of what I saw, to blocking what I did not want to see, and now to asking and receiving a mental image. I have now advanced to the stage that some visions are accompanied by a "circle of light" because I was taught to ask for its protection. Most of the time I receive a symbolic image, but sometimes I receive a psychic message in regard to a question asked. It is, as defined by Gwenn, my closest and dearest friend, an exploration into the spiritual world. She is the one who has had faith in me and has encouraged me to develop this gift. She has also been able to interpret the visions that I see when I cannot. Most visions I receive need her divine counsel.

In addition to describing psychic mental images as visions, I also speak of Gods, angels and guides. I use the terms interchangeably, and sometimes within the same description. Since I cannot reasonably discern between them, I site whatever feels most comfortable at each point of writing. I truly believe, that in whatever form they appear to be, they are undoubtedly an invincible energy and are probably created from the same powerful source.

All of my writing is based on fact and truth as I believe it to be. Much of it is as much a mystery to me as I hope it is to my readers. As I learn more, I continue to write of my unceasing journey of discovery.

Occasionally I am able to interpret what is presented to me symbolically on my own, without Gwenn's divine assistance. Only this morning I reviewed a vision that I had seen months earlier and now am able to assign an interpretation to this image. It was a representation of my cousin as a skeleton, whose arms and legs were suspended by strings like that of a marionette. I could see that Cheryl did not have control of her own life and that parts of it were vacant and brittle. She was being directed in a spiritual way to accomplish some purpose.

I then took it one step further. I asked this visionary image where it came from and saw the form of Aunt Jenny, the person whose spirit is connected with the reincarnated soul and vision of my cousin, Cheryl.

I now saw the family lineage that has carried this spirit on. The next question is to find out what she is all about, what her purpose is, and what will allow her to rest in peace. This restless spirit and others are defined herein.

Many characters in this book are carried over from their introduction in "Visual Encounters." It is not necessary that you have this background, but it might give a more complete description of a particular person's character. I also wish to state at this time that while I had referenced times of a poor relationship with my mother in the section "About the Author," I have now come to a spiritual understanding of the underlying causes for her behavior. The reasons are the culmination of many psychic messages received and latent, intuitive insight. I gladly give complete explanation of my spiritual journey in this writing of "Unraveling the Weave."

CHAPTER ONE

Unraveling the Weave

At a time when my life was under extreme stress, I had three distinct visions come clearly into view in my mind's eye. I was in the midst of divorce and could feel the loss of my family and home. I was unable to capture a good night's rest. One night, while trying to sleep, these three visions came to me in slow motion, close-up, and sequentially.

The first was of a dark-skinned woman with a broad smile. The second was of white, galloping horses. The third, and the one I will address more fully, was of three tombstones.

The tombstones were set within a gravesite somewhere and were adroitly pointed out to me by a spirit that illuminated itself like a fluorescent tube as it outlined the specific tombstones I was to see. Two were in close proximity of each other, and the spirit ran up one side of the tombstone, over the top, and down the other side before going to the next. The third was located some distance away and the spirit had to travel far to find and illuminate the outline of the last tombstone.

For years I felt that what I had seen were pure hallucinations. There seemed no other logic or reason for them, but I never forgot them. In recent years, however, I have assigned purpose to their existence and have expended enormous effort to define what they are about. Following are my thoughts.

In analyzing the persons in my family, I find that the strength of some of their personalities deserve scrutiny. There is evidence of spirits who are at unrest and their needs have not yet been satisfied. Their purposes are not yet defined and I feel the roots of their dissatisfaction lie restless perhaps under the tombstones that I saw in my secondary vision. An analogy might be like being buried alive, knowing some injustice had been done, and not having the opportunity for reparation.

These restless spirits project themselves by various means and sometimes in eccentric ways. I find them to exert themselves by using extreme patterns of behavior. They must be in painful states, carrying a captive evil that is fighting to be free. I have identified them as attaching themselves to specific members of my family and have arbitrarily assigned them as belonging to each of the three souls whose headstones I have seen. I believe these souls were buried without restitution.

I may never find out the stories of the tragedies that lie with those buried souls, or determine which attribute belongs specifically to each, but I feel the need to identify them and their purposes. Once identified, I know that each family member currently plagued with them and their given mission must address the issues to allow these spirits to rest in peace.

I now feel I am able to take you along the path that I have taken to *unravel the weave*.

CHAPTER TWO

Mystique

I was with my daughter, Sue. We were having a leisurely Saturday morning, having docked our boat at the riverfront marina. It was a wonderful place to be, with the sun shining and the air warm. We had spent the night on the boat after hearing a free concert the night before which had been played in a gazebo on the bank of the Chase River. These concerts take place every Friday evening of the summer, and are sponsored by the city and a popular beverage company.

Sue is a self-assured girl in her mid-twenties. She's a pretty brunette and keeps herself well. She attracts many with her outgoing and zestful personality. She is at this time, however, finding it difficult to put herself back comfortably into a dating situation after having recently lost her husband. Because of this, she and I have developed a friend relationship as well as mother-to-daughter.

Following Sue's lead, we shopped in the downtown area of this city of Mt. Carmel. This is the largest city near my home. There were so many places to shop and eat, including the wonderful gourmet coffee shop where we had delightful baked goods with our morning coffee. We then ventured through an open farmer's market and gathered fresh flowers, herbs and vegetables. In our wandering through the stores, Sue bought a casual summer dress at a small boutique to use as a bathing suit cover-up and I, a hanging lamp at a second-hand store.

We stopped to have lunch at an outdoor pub, and sat in the sunshine on bar stools at a high table. We each had salads and drinks and, without trying, Sue managed to attract the attention of males who watched her with noted interest.

After lunch, we went into another little shop I had not even known was in town. It was actually a psychic store that had a limited selection of books, crystals and other objects which were used as vehicles to converse with the spirits. I casually glanced at book titles, occasionally looking through one for its contents. I was searching for something that would be key to identifying the imagery I was able to see but found nothing. I called this mental imagery "visions," but could find no identification in writing with anyone having a similar experience.

In conversation with a young man behind the counter, I inquired as to the knowledge of such information and if there were any books on the subject within the store. The young man turned out to be the store owner's son. He said that he knew exactly what I wanted and began to search the shelves for such a book. Finding nothing, he apologized, and said he did not have anything of that nature within the store at this time.

"Well," I said, "I really don't understand what it is that I see as it is all given to me symbolically."

"Yes, of course," said the man behind the counter assuredly. "Spirits must converse this way or use some other vehicle in order to reach you."

Still somewhat disbelieving in myself, I left the store with a more keen interest in finding out about this gift. These spirits certainly had their own mystique.

CHAPTER THREE

Interpreting a Vision

One day, while having a shower, I began thinking about my cousin, Cheryl, and the image I saw of her as a dancing skeleton. In my mental vision, the skeleton's arms and legs were suspended by strings, like that of a marionette. Along with that vision I saw another with a set of skeletal jaws, belonging to Shelly, one of her daughters.

I had grown up closely with Cheryl having lived across the street from her until about age eight. In our teen years, even though she and her parents had moved away, we still were both cousin and friend. When I visited her or saw her at family functions, I envied her slim figure, attractiveness, and maturity with boys.

Cheryl's mother had always been the more attractive of the two sisters. My mother was rather plain. It was little wonder that Cheryl would become an attractive young woman. I felt unattractive, immature and awkward next to her.

As the years passed, Cheryl's life became less enviable. She lost her Mom when she was barely a newlywed, later divorced, remarried unsuccessfully, and divorced again. She had four children, and struggled to raise them through these hardships. I dare say the hardships took their toll on her, and the second divorce left her feeling flawed and marked. She was somewhat embarrassed about these circumstances, though she need not have been considering how commonplace subsequent divorces are today.

My interpretation of this puppet vision was simply that Cheryl never had control of her own life. She was the carrier and reincarnation of another soul, just as a psychic had told her some years ago. The psychic actually showed her that she carried two sets of finger prints in her hands.

By this vision I doubted if she would ever gain control in this lifetime. My assumption was that her daughter, portrayed to me as "the jaws," had also inherited the "mouth" of this reincarnated soul. She would be carrying this same, unsettled spirit unless satisfied.

I told Gwenn of this interpretation in regard to Cheryl and got general agreement. Gwenn was my closest friend who had been the catalyst in getting me to pay attention to the mental images and uncertain powers that I had. This was one instance of very few that Gwenn was unable to define for me. Most of the time she gave me implicit interpretation of the visions I received. I seemed to be inept in determining what was meant by the symbolism of these strange and obscure messages.

Gwenn added that the spirit was beginning to enter Cheryl's daughter, Shelly. She felt it was apparent that Cheryl would not complete the task in this lifetime, and that Shelly would have to carry it out and resolve its purpose. I had to agree, as those strings most certainly had control of the skeleton puppet.

I imagined that I should explain my visions and interpretations to Cheryl in order for her to find some internal answer, but I doubted she would have the capacity to believe or the spiritual level to understand this intangible concept.

While in the shower that day, seeing this manipulated skeleton in my mind's eye, I asked "Where are you from? Why are you here?" And a vision of a dark-haired lady appeared. I felt she had dark eyes like Cheryl's Aunt Jenny, her father's sister, and then knew that this spirit was somehow connected with Aunt Jenny who is still alive.

I can see that this unsettled spirit is being passed down from generation to generation in her family. Maybe some day the timing will be right to ask her what it is that she needs.

CHAPTER FOUR

My Father's Visit

It was very early in the morning. I had awakened, but was still in bed. I was aware of something going on up above me. Someone was watching me. It was my father. Rob had brought him to me and was there, too. I did not move.

Rob was my daughter's late husband who had died of suicide only a couple of months previous. He was very much on our minds.

I felt so stupid. Here I was, a grown woman lying in bed, with my father watching me. It almost felt humiliating, but I understood. He had wanted to see his daughter, and Rob had helped him. I just lay there letting him soak me in, for what felt like an eternity. I did not stare back, as I didn't want to terminate the process and thought that it might.

My Dad had been deceased for about thirty years, and although I had missed him dearly, I had never felt his presence until now. I have, however, been awakened from time to time by someone shaking my bed or nudging me. I often wondered if it might be him, but I never knew why. I never thought to ask.

My Aunt Addie used to comment on someone sometimes shaking her bed as she slept, too. Since my Dad was her brother, my thought was that it might be him in both instances, but she surely didn't know either.

I later learned that the spirits that shake my bed during the night are those that have not fully crossed over. They are harmless, but definitely a nuisance. They can be told to go away. Perhaps they are still around because their work was not done and their purposes may not have been satisfied.

Brenda, my Tarot card reader, feels as though my house is a gateway for spirits. She always finds it easy to give readings in my house. That does not explain why Aunt Addie has spirits that shake her bed or why she was able to see her deceased husband and a lady visit her during the night.

So there I was, being watched. I can just imagine how this all came about, too. Rob had met up with my father in heaven and said, "Oh, yeah, I know her. I know where she is, too. I can take you to her."

That would be just what Rob would do. He was such an amicable guy and could talk with anyone. I remember Sue telling me of an incident that happened at a nearby discount store. They had gone in to do some shopping, and a girl in the store was having an argument with a salesgirl in one of the aisles. Sue went on about her business and got out of the way. Rob, on the other hand, got into the middle of the discussion and tried to be mediator to the situation. He wanted to help them work out their differences.

There were many instances in which Rob embarrassed Sue with his assertive and congenial nature. This was one of them, even though she could later appreciate how comical the situation had been. Looking back, it is this ease, this no compunction or apprehension with a given situation, that is a definite sign of a bi-polar disorder.

I recognized it even then, of course; and why wouldn't I. I was quite familiar with the characteristics. But I thought of these elements as 'personality traits' and certainly not dangerous. I never pinpointed it to an illness, just Rob's personality.

Matt had been diagnosed as having a manic-depressive illness to his total life's upheaval. He displayed quite similar characteristics. I later learned that this was also known as bi-polar disorder.

Matt was my steady man of long tenure. He and I had gone to lunch one day in Canada, and he had overheard a couple discuss that it was their anniversary. When we got up to leave, Matt picked up the tab for the celebrating couple's lunch. All I could say was, "That was very manic of you." It was a wonderful gesture, I agreed, but not one I thought of as exactly normal.

Rob's mother had suffered from the disorder for many years, and when Sue met with her physician, he had commented that she was the most severe case he had ever seen. I'm not so sure I agree with that, but she certainly was a classic case. She suffered from alternate states of depression to euphoric highs. I had seen her during the most severely depressed state, where she hardly took care of herself and had to be hospitalized, to her coming out of it to be the most beautiful woman I had ever seen. She captured the eyes and hearts of everyone around her.

Matt never showed any signs of depression. He had been told that he consistently experienced his highs and lows within the same moment. I suspect that Rob may have encountered similar cycles. While not ever having been diagnosed, I'm sad to say that a bi-polar disorder is probably the reason he took his life. Shortly after his marriage to my daughter, a severe depression set in and he was in total despair.

After Rob's suicide, Matt took a step back and avoided getting close to the situation. Knowing that Matt had been diagnosed with the same illness set me back a distance, too. I began to question if I wanted to stay in a relationship with someone who may have this potential capability.

In years past, Matt had been right there to assist me with any crisis in my life, but he was staying clear of me now. The reason was probably twofold: he was getting close to an ensuing divorce and had been showing signs of not wanting to make a commitment to me; but more importantly, the actuality of someone having the same disorder performing a suicide was just too painful. He wanted no part of this heart-breaking, incomprehensible situation. We eventually parted ways, but for other reasons. Matt claimed he needed an intermission.

CHAPTER FIVE

In Touch with the Spirits

It must be only during certain times that we are able to be in touch with the spirits. When life is too busy, and we are too active to notice, we are not aware of them-- but they are always there. Sometimes, when more attuned, or in touch, things happen that are remotely obvious and I take notice. You will see by the excerpts that follow that they are always present. One must learn to be open to receiving these messages.

Steve
For instance, upon meeting Steve and dating him about the second or third time, I looked at his face, at his physique, and I knew that I had known him. He had been in my life sometime before, but not this lifetime. There was a familiarity, an all too mysterious familiarity, and I knew his soul had traveled somewhere before with mine, in some other life. He had returned to complete whatever role there was to play out with me now. There is an uncanny closeness and attraction that I feel, but because of the deliberate distance and separateness that Steve places in this relationship, I continue to be patient and await his cue and comfort. I am stumbling over the word comfort, for Steve is anything but comfortable in the relationship. I believe he is hurting too badly over the loss of a marriage and pending loss of his ailing mother.

<u>TMX 582</u>

I was driving on the freeway to meet Gwenn for dinner, and I spotted a license plate which read TMX 582. Often times I read license plates for psychic messages. I instinctively knew this was a message regarding Aunt Addie, and I smiled at the subtlety in which the message was presented. TMX was definitely "Timex," the brand name of one of her watches that she had given me shortly before she was placed in the nursing home. By this message she was telling me that "It was time to come and see her." The numbers 5, 8 and 2 were present on the plate, and something I read to be: "5," mutual (meeting), "8," of a heightened or ultimate experience, and "2," of sharing. The message was quite clear, and I made a mental plan to see her within the next day or two.

<u>Rob's Spirit</u>

In this same time frame, the pendulum clock in my dining area, for the second time now in its approximate 20 year history with me was malfunctioning. When Rob, my daughter's late husband, came into her life some two years prior to their getting married, the clock stopped working properly. It still kept time, but the pendulum would not swing. The clock was not out of balance; it had been placed upon two screws which were securely affixed into the wall, making it impossible for the clock to tilt in one direction or the other. During Sue and Rob's entire relationship and short marriage, this same condition prevailed. Even with new batteries, the pendulum would not swing.

Upon Rob's death, four timepieces in my house stopped working: two watches, the small battery clock in my bathroom, and this kitchen clock. (Rob's own watch, however, with a built-in alarm set to go off at the time he would get up to go to work still worked fine. The alarm, which Sue could not figure out how to turn off, continued to ring.) The battery clock in my bathroom was discarded as it was not repairable. One of the two watches required a new battery; the other was not battery-operated and was repaired. A new set of batteries were placed in the kitchen clock--and the pendulum began to swing as it once had.

This pendulum has swung for a year and a half and now has suddenly stopped. Its stopping coincided with the day of Brenda's card readings of some girls, one at a time, in my kitchen. No efforts of rebalancing, hand starting, or coaxing will make this clock work properly at this time. Sue had been over this day as well, but she did not have her cards read. Gwenn believes Sue brought Rob's spirit into the house again. The upcoming week is to be Sue's deposition in regard to a wrongful death suit in his behalf. The medical profession had failed to act upon or treat his obvious and openly admitted depressed state which resulted in a suicidal death. Rob was heavy in her heart and in her soul.

Aunt Addie's Hat

Of course, when the clock stopped, I was concerned about my Aunt Addie. I have heard that a clock's stopping and death have been related by some reportings, so I thought of her and quickly looked at the hat on my opposite kitchen wall. She had given this hat to me and from it I take occasional readings as to her condition.

While suffering from Alzheimer's and living in a nursing home, her spirit is somehow readable to me through that small straw hat. It takes on a light and fluffy look when I feel she is happy, and the lace seems to droop and look drab when things are not well with her.

One day the hat appeared to be trying to tell me something about her unrestful condition, but I did not have the time to go see her that day. I later learned that she had taken it upon herself to walk out of the nursing home to go shopping. She was found by her daughter-in-law, several agonizing hours later, pushing a shopping cart at a nearby shopping mall.

I believe she was angry with me because I had not gone to see her and had not taken her shopping. Her disposition was such that if she became tired of waiting for someone to do something for her, she would take care of it herself. So it was! She took herself shopping.

The Card Reading
The day Brenda was over to read Tarot cards, she read mine and gave me specific statements, the first of which was about Steve and went like this:

> There is a man in your life who is undecided about something in regard to you. He has decided not to make a decision. He has decided not to decide. He is in too much pain, and has been hurt too badly to open up to any feelings with you. He is 'driving you up a wall' (and he was), but he is in a state of

numbness, and cannot feel any emotion. I feel you will go along with this until about October, and then you will confront him. There may even be a confrontation. You will address the situation and tell him he must open up or go away until he decides he wants to open up with you. This will be good, because he will then begin to get in touch with his feelings.

The Arrival of the Dove

Spending more time at home these days and enjoying the view of the lake from my home, I see that a bird has joined me in the yard. Because it does not fly away at my appearance, I suspect that it is hurt and hungry. My next-door neighbor, Karen, also noticed the bird. We discussed what kind of bird it might be, but neither of us really knew. It stayed all day, and I fed it some bread.

That evening, my daughter stopped by and, upon seeing the bird said, "Why, that's a Morning Dove," and began to "coo" at it. It responded to her by tilting its head and intently listening to her sounds. When she said it was a dove, I instinctively knew it was Matt's spirit that had come to see me. Matt had kept a dove as a pet in his home for 10 years.

I reasoned that this spirit had come at this time because of the upcoming deposition Sue was to have in regard to Rob's death. I thought perhaps it had come to watch over us. Sue and Matt shared a special kind of father-to-daughter relationship and understanding as well. In fact, at one point when Matt and I decided to break off the relationship, it was Sue that cried.

I noticed that one of my two electronic clocks in the kitchen had stopped at 10:15 a.m. It is not uncommon for the power to go off at my house from time to time, but it is uncommon for only one clock to stop. It was the one on the microwave and not the stove. I supposed the bird had come at 10:15 a.m.

I called Gwenn the following day and left her a message on her office voice mail. I wanted to tell her about the bird and that it had stayed the night sleeping on top of the cover of my patio table. It was still there when I awoke, and it stayed in the yard all day.

At 9:00 a.m. the next morning, the telephone rang. It was Gwenn, who had just returned to the office from an out-of-town trip. She had listened to my message and had called to say, "He's not there to help you. He's there to spy on you!"

She followed up to say that it would be extremely rare for a bird to sleep in an unprotected area like on a table. It was their instinct to stay better protected. They preferred to be far out on a limb of a tree, where the weight of a predator, such as a cat, would not be supported.

When children or the neighbor's dog came into the yard, the bird flew up to the top of the fence or gazebo, but it did not leave.

I told Gwenn that Matt's spirit was leaving its droppings on my table. We chuckled at the implications of this.

The next day the bird was on the grass in my neighbor's yard, which was separated from mine by a fence. When I went outside on my deck, the bird saw me and got very excited. I thought this a very strange thing for a stray bird. It maneuvered itself back and forth on the ground, trying to get to me through that fence. I was in a hurry to go somewhere, and returned to the inside of my home to finish getting ready.

I didn't see the bird the following day, but the next day the painter had shown up and was working outside on the far side of my house. As I was circling the perimeter of my house to see him, I spotted the dove on the ground. It had died in my yard. I provided Don a double plastic bag and a shovel, and asked him to dispose of the bird. He reluctantly agreed to do this chore.

When I could pull Gwenn aside from the next breakfast meeting of friends, I asked her for her interpretation. She answered, "He had come to see if he could get back in, and finding he could not, died of a broken heart."

I later relayed the story of the dove to a few other friends at a gathering at my house. I did not mention a potential relationship to any spirit. I just spoke of the incident of the bird running back and forth on the ground on the other side of the fence and later finding it dead in my yard. The unsolicited statement was that "It had died of a broken heart."

CHAPTER SIX

You're in My Face

My friend, Matt, had made his separation from me over a year ago. It was quite painful for us both, but something he felt compelled to do. His words were always carefully selected in order to give the clearest meaning of what he thought and felt. I trusted him implicitly.

After a year's separation, with a few interactions handled by fate, I learned that he had gone on with his life with another woman. I felt heart broken and betrayed.

"Gwenn, I said, I need an interpretation." Gwenn was my sole interpreter of the many visions I received.

"What's that?" she queried.

"I'm now angry with Matt. I no longer think about him, and I don't want to see him. I don't want to deal with him. If I saw him on the street, I would ignore him. I'm angry."

Matt had been such a special man in my life, and one whom I had learned to love deeply. After fourteen years together, he found it necessary, for karmic reasons, to take leave. I also believe I was partially responsible for driving him away with my apparent "power" over him in his recently divorced and weakened state.

"Remember the vision I had seen of him in the water with his head resting on a board? And he was just observing like a bump on a log? Well, he's doing the same thing, but he's not in the water. He's huge, and he's in my face! What does it mean?"

He is very disturbed about you and wants to get your attention," she said.

"Why?" I asked.

"Because you have gone on with your life, or you have the potential to go on."

"Ooohh," I said. "That's why he's in my face. How does he know?"

"Because your souls are connected. I told you that."

I had been dating Steve who was a very promising gentleman, had great potential and was very attracted to me.

"Here's something else," I said. Remember when I had that telepathic spiritual talk with him while sitting on my couch, and I asked him if I should go on with my life? And later that evening, while eating dinner, my hand became his? Our souls were one. Now, my hand hurts every day like I may have some arthritis in it, but only my left hand. That's the one that he held. Does he want me to let go?"

"No, he doesn't want you to let go. Maybe he's clinching his fist in anger and doesn't want to let go of you. Try clinching your fist and see if it hurts."

"No," I said, as I tried it. "It usually hurts most in the morning, but sometimes it aches during the day."

"Do this," she said. "The next time it hurts, tell him to let go."

CHAPTER SEVEN

An Unwelcome Respite

Steve and I had been dating consistently once a week for the past six months, and I do mean dating. A real romance was not part of this scenario. I presumed this was because he was still in the process of divorce and unable to release that type of emotion with me. Additionally, he was just as likely to be afraid of the involvement. In any regard, I accepted the terms offered because of the attraction I felt toward him and the good times we shared in going out.

With the last holiday, which he spent at his cottage with his boys, he stopped calling me. I knew in my heart that there was nothing really wrong between he and I, but because of whatever was going on with him, he was unable to carry on a dating relationship with me at this time.

My friends encouraged me to call him, but I was reluctant, until the perfect reason presented itself at the most appropriate time.

Steve had a wicker dinette set and one of the four chairs had a broken leg. He had asked me if I knew anyone who could fix furniture. I had told him that the person I knew was now living in Florida and when he came into town this summer, I would ask him.

On Friday I got a call from Graham, who said he had come in from Florida the previous week. He asked if he could come over on Sunday. "Of course," I said, and I asked him about fixing Steve's chair. He said he didn't bring any tools with him, but he knew a shop where he could take it and would fix it. I should get the chair to my house and he would pick it up when he came over.

Thus, I had the perfect reason to call Steve. Although Steve and I have never had a good telephone relationship, and only brief conversations, we talked for an hour and a half. He was definitely glad to hear from me, and I deliberately let the conversation go on for as long as he wanted to carry it out. Upon closing, although somewhat positive, he left me with a heavy heart.

He said, "I think we should get together again, maybe later on in the summer. How's that?" That was not what I really wanted to hear, but obviously was what he needed. With this question, he was checking to see if I was still going to be interested later on.

In my most positive voice, I indicated that would be fine. I knew he didn't need any additional pressure on him, but was sad for the rest of the night.

He agreed he would drop off the chair and we set the date and time.

CHAPTER EIGHT

A Definite Sign

I was driving to my friend, Patty's, house to pick her up for dinner. My right hand began to hurt. I loosened my grip on the steering wheel to see if I had caused the discomfort by gripping it too tightly. I decided that I had not. I remembered that about nine or ten years ago I had cut one of my hands pretty badly on a broken ceramic lamp, and the cut had left a scar. I looked to see which hand that had been. The scar was in my left palm, not the hand that was hurting.

It continued to hurt, with the feeling that a tendon was drawing the palm of my hand closed. I looked at my hand to see if I could see anything. It looked slightly like that may be happening, but I really could not be sure. I did note to myself that Steve had a problem with his right hand where the tendon visually drew his hand closed, and he was concerned that it may become a problem for him to play the piano. Aside from his full-time profession, he loved his music.

I then knew that this was a sign, a positive sign, and it concerned Steve. It continued to hurt and draw in for the remainder of the hour, and then again later in the evening. I knew I would mention it to Gwenn and ask her for her interpretation of this sign. It did not hurt at all during the time I spent heavily engaged in conversation with Patty.

When I spoke to Gwenn the following day, I told her of my experience and that I felt it was due to some connection with Steve. "Yes," she said. "It isn't so much a sign as it is the indication that you are probably able to communicate telepathically with Steve."

"Oh," I said. "Do you mean that because Steve's hand hurts, my hand hurts? Or if he is trying to send me a message I'll know because my hand hurts like his does?"

"Uh huh," she said.

"What is it with me and the hands?" I asked. "Matt was able to touch my hand, too, when I communicated telepathically with him."

CHAPTER NINE

You've Touched My Heart

I was pensive for the next few days, awaiting the time for Steve to deliver his broken chair to my house. We had decided he would come over one morning before he went to work. I had lunch plans with a girl I used to work with, so I wanted to be dressed and ready to go as soon as Steve left. He knew I had to leave by 11:00 a.m.

When Steve arrived, I had received a call from another girlfriend, and was still on the phone when the doorbell rang. I carried the portable phone with me, continuing my conversation as I opened the door and waved to Steve to come in.

He wore a broad smile as he always did, and came in. He put his hand out as if to want to shake hands, and I extended mine. With that, he pulled me toward him and gave me a hug. I told Kristen to hold, and with arms held out, said "Come here," to Steve. He willingly embraced me again with a bigger, more compassionate hug, and kissed me. I ended my conversation with Kristen.

I asked Steve if he had time for a coffee, and he said that he did. I poured a cup for each of us, and we decided to take our coffee outside and drink it on the patio. He loved to look out at the lake and enjoy the scenery, and also the landscaping I had done in the yard.

He picked up the cup of coffee, became entranced at something in the kitchen, and poured the coffee all over himself and the floor, hardly recognizing it. I could see he was an "emotional mess." I made no fuss about it and grabbed some paper toweling to address both him and the floor. I then poured another cup of coffee for him and we went outside.

We had an enjoyable hour-long light conversation out on the patio. Upon his leaving, he put the broken chair in my garage. I explained that I would call him when I got his chair back which should be the following week. He got into his car to leave saying, "I'll be talking to you."

I was not about to let him leave without a more expressive statement of how I felt about him. With due care not to alarm or scare him, I started out with, "I miss you."

He smiled, and was visibly "all over the place" emotionally. Leaning into his car so he could not escape, I said "Did you hear me?" and sweetly added again, . . . "I miss you."

"Oh, we'll be getting together again," he said nervously and with a bright smile, almost laughing. Humor is always what he needed to get through any emotional circumstance.

"You do whatever it is you need to do," I said, with a reassuring pause.

"Oh, that's just what I'm doing," he said positively and

with an apprehensive counter.

"I just want you to know that you have touched my heart," I continued.

He broke in to lightheartedly interject. "And I'll keep touching it," he said.

"And," I continued, smiling at his response, "I do miss you." To relieve his tension, and let him know that I understood, I placed my hand on his cheek, kissed him gently and said, "You take care."

"I will," he said, and I turned to leave him, so he could freely pull out of the driveway. I could see he received my message well and we would be all right. I had never openly expressed any emotion with him, other than a moment of passion wherein I was abruptly halted by his humor. I felt he needed to hear something about my feelings for him at this time. Perhaps those tender words would carry him through some difficult times.

CHAPTER TEN

Unable to Bring a Vision Forward

I've been concerned about Aunt Addie, who has Alzheimer's disease and is living in a nursing home. I have been unable to see her spiritual vision for a few days now. What I had seen recently was a bed of vibrantly colored spring flowers, with sunlight so brilliant that it must have been heaven itself. But now, I cannot see the flowers, their brightness, or vivid color. Once I thought I could see a couple of weakly standing flowers, wilting, and having little life left in them.

My concern is that Aunt Addie may be near death. I knew that she did not have much of a life in her current state, but I wasn't ready to let her go. She has been pretty close to death before, with her heart stopping a couple of times, but her spiritual vision did not change. In fact, when the disease was setting in is when I believe this new assigned image came into being.

I expressed my concern to Gwenn. She thought perhaps her Alzheimer's may have been particularly bad on the days I tried to view her vision and that was my problem. I have already proven that I can take an up-to-the-day reading of someone by checking their assigned symbolic image in my mind's eye.

Dark-Skinned Lady

CHAPTER ELEVEN

Pieces of a Puzzle

Some time ago now, during my divorce, is when I had those three consecutive and unforgettable visions. At that time I termed them as hallucinations.

My attorney had just told me to give my marital home to my ex-husband-to-be, and I was enraged at him. It was one of those terribly disconcerting nights where I could not sleep peacefully.

I distinctly remember seeing three separate, slow-motion mental videos in full color. Each frame stayed in place for a very long time before going to the next. The first was of a dark-skinned lady, with a pleasant, broad smile and round face.

As I tried to study the face, it zoomed closer and larger for me to see. I believe she wore a headdress, which was very difficult to see. I could only see a mere shadow of white across the top of her head. I later saw a picture of an Indian with a headdress of what appeared to be what this lady in my vision was wearing. It had dark feathers at the base which would have blended in with her dark hair. A small row of white feathers ran across the top, like the narrow band I could see in her hair. As I studied her, a more close-up view appeared, and her smile broadened.

Gwenn thought because her face was round and full that perhaps she was Aztec.

White, Galloping Horses

The second vision followed immediately and was of white, galloping horses. I studied the horses carefully. I stirred and tried to sleep again.

The third vision now came into view. It took place in a graveyard. I looked upon the two tombstones before me when a live spirit moved its way through, and with deliberation, carefully illuminated the rounded tops of the headstones, one at a time. The spirit pointed out three headstones in total. It found the first two located relatively close to one another, but had to travel some distance to find the third. When it did, it proceeded to again illuminate its outline.

I felt I was being shown the three for some purpose, but could not imagine why. I felt as though I had seen portions of my past lives, even then, as I tried to put some sense into what I had seen. I was aware of having a heightened sense about me from the stress of divorce.

While it has been my goal to unravel the weave of the various spiritual aspects of my life, my discoveries linger in abeyance for long periods of time. I have harbored these three images for more than ten years and have only recently felt that I've been able to satisfy some reasons for their existence.

Since I rarely remember my dreams and sometimes wonder if I even have them, these three visions have posed more than an idle curiosity. I believe they may be connected to the restless spirits in my family's lineage and are clues to defining what they are about. They

Three Tombstones

were pointed out to me to resolve their mysteries, and I have taken them on as my mission.

Since these spirits are in a restless state they need to be addressed. I even think, now, that whoever shakes my bed at night, which I've been told are beings that have not fully crossed over, are these spirits that need to be satisfied. They have haunted the women in my family for years.

Perhaps the dark-skinned woman and the galloping horses will give clues at some point to dark stories of the past, but I believe their foundation, the reasons they still exist, lie beneath the three tombstones. I will even go as far as to say that they are the spirits that my stepdad referred to at my mother's death when he said, "She will finally be rid of the demons that possessed her."

CHAPTER TWELVE

Metamorphosis

It was now customary for me to casually check on known spiritual visions I had learned to see and accept. From time to time, as the person entered my mind, I also took the opportunity to look at their spirit.

The next vision I checked was Gwenn's. The angel, once flitting around, spreading good tidings to all, had turned black. It was now lying in the rubble. It danced no more, sparkled no more, and appeared to be fading away.

A metamorphosis, I felt. I'm awaiting a new image of Gwenn to appear, but I somehow feel that a change is taking place for her. Perhaps her life's focus will no longer be helping other people, and she will be able to concentrate on her own life and well being. It is much needed.

Not only do I feel a metamorphosis for Gwenn, but also for my daughter, Sue. And then, there is Aunt Addie whose vision I can no longer bring in to my mind's eye. At present I'm actually afraid to check for any others. I'm not sure I like change in this spiritual respect any more than I like it in real life. It is not comfortable.

Days have passed, and I've deliberately not checked others' spiritual visions. I'm not sure I want to know what is going on. However, at some point this evening I did see Gwenn's friend Derek and his wife, in my mind's eye, and they were still represented by salt and pepper shakers. They were a pair, but as different as black and white. Their dance was no longer a "soft shoe" or "wedding dance," however; I guess I might now describe it as a "jig." That was a relief. Not everything was changing in its entirety--only in time as governing factors changed.

The circumstances that surrounded their relationship were that they were at the end of their marriage. It was nearing the Christmas holidays when I first saw this vision, so they were treating each other with some delicacy (soft shoe), and also were somewhat melancholy (wedding dance) over their marriage. I sensed that the marriage would not last long into the new year, and now the "jig" was indicating a faster pace toward the end.

The three spiritual visions that are changing, thus far, make me feel that it may be due to some planetary influence; however, I know nothing about astrological forces, so can't expound on it. I just find it very strange that three of my closest contacts are in a state of fluctuation.

The dictionary describes change as a transformation, as by magic or sorcery. A marked change in appearance, character, condition or function. A change in structure or habits. I find it very peculiar that a dictionary can give one spiritual explanation when it was not written with this intent at all.

CHAPTER THIRTEEN

Unresolved Spirits

In discussions with Gwenn, while analyzing particular incidences that have occurred within my family, we again agree there are three evil spirits still present. I alluded to their tie-in with the vision I had of the three tombstones in the graveyard. I did not come to this realization for many years, but have since reasoned they were spiritually pointed out to me intentionally.

I have identified these family spirits. The first is with my grandmother, who is represented to me as a cat with eerie emerald-green eyes. This demon has worked its way through the generations down to my daughter. The second, I believe, is with my cousin, Cheryl, whom I have seen as a dancing skeleton with puppet strings. The third belongs to my mother, who has shown herself to me as a dragon.

Certainly each has its own supernatural and extraordinary implication. Each of these women have had alternate and intermittent incredibly mean dispositions when they were otherwise pleasant individuals. I have seen this meanness carried out by my cousin, but never by her mother. I have also seen it carried out by my grandmother, my mother, myself, and now by my daughter.

It is a fact that we each carry a strain of Indian blood from the Crow tribe. From what I have read, this particular breed of Indian can have a mean disposition.

Somehow, although I'm judging myself, I would like to think that most of the meanness has stopped with me. I have outgrown its ugliness with the mellowing of age, but my grandmother and mother never did. The spirit erupts during times of extreme stress, and my daughter has had witness to it herself. It appears when she is frustrated, has been irresponsible about something or perhaps is disappointed in herself.

To define these spirits, I'll begin with the simplest because Cheryl offered it to me. It is something that was told to her in a Tarot card reading. A woman who looked at her hands told her that she was a reincarnated soul. She was also told that her purpose in this life was to learn "independence." I feared that she would not learn this lesson in this lifetime, but considerable time has passed, and she is well on her way to success.

Ironically, Cheryl has nearly severed her relationship with me. I am left to assume that it may be a step in earning her "independence," so I am letting her go at this time. I am glad to report that she and Sue do share a good relationship.

Because of seeing the skeletal jaws of one of her daughters, I believe it is this independence that must also be carried out by Shelly. This would be a reasonable mission as she is the one who appears to be the most dependent of all four children. That may also be her purpose in this lifetime.

One day, while discussing something with Gwenn about my grandmother's evil spirit, she said to me, "Ask her what her purpose is."

"Ask my grandmother?" I said.

"Yes, ask her. Ask her what she wants."

When I remembered, I meditated one night before going to sleep. I asked my grandmother what her purpose was. A psychic message came forth as she tried to explain it to me, but I was very sleepy and her answer became hazy to me by morning.

"Did you ask her?" Gwenn later questioned me.

"Yes, I did. I unfortunately was very sleepy, but it had something to do with power."

"Power," she said. "That's very interesting. You are a commanding person. I can see how the power fits with you."

"Yes," I agreed. I often worried about the extent of the power I had. While never practiced, one time I had even confided in Matt that I felt I had the power within me to make evil things happen. He had agreed with me.

In discussion with Sue and Gwenn over dinner one evening, I reiterated my feeling that the three unresolved spirits were connected to the tombstones I had seen in the graveyard of my mental vision. I expressed that I felt I understood one spirit to be with my cousin, and its purpose was "independence," and the other, which I learned psychically from my grandmother's spirit, stood for "power." I had not made any connection to the ruthless traits that were shared by my grandmother, my mother, myself and my daughter. I did feel, however, that the third spirit was a demon that belonged to my mother.

"I don't know what my mother's spiritual purpose is," I stated. "She appeared to me as a dragon, but a dragon could be friendly, hateful, protective, fierce, or even bring good luck." It left me at a loss and without confirmation.

Sue stated she felt it had something to do with "love," as she felt my mother had not known how to love unconditionally. She felt that because my mother failed in her relationship with me, that her spirit was still restless.

Her words were probably a truism, but I couldn't fathom a restless spirit representing "love." It did not feel comfortable to me and I didn't believe it was the true definition of this spirit. I did not perish the thought, however.

I have now pondered this dilemma for a few years, with still no more insight. One day, upon having a passing thought to ask for more definition, a *spiritual message* told me that the undefined spirit had something to do with "protect," but at this time I'm not sure about that given information either. It does not denote evil any more than "love," and I feel evil is very much a part of its existence.

I just had a flashback of a message I received from reading the letters and numbers of a license plate. This particular message came to me some time ago while driving, and while looking at various license plates of cars I passed or that passed me. I often read them and received messages from the combination of letters and numbers on the plates.

The message was "protect," but I knew at the time that I did not attach it to any specific letters or numbers of any one particular license plate that I had seen. My interpretation at that time was that I was to be "protective" of something, but I didn't know of what. My feeling now is that I must have had a passing thought in regard to this spiritual quest, and I had been given an answer. I just didn't make the connection.

Still in a quandary about this unnamed spirit, I reviewed what I did feel I knew about all three. I said to myself, "So now we have "power," "independence" and maybe "love" or "protect." I feel it is my mission to discover what these spirits are all about and thereby resolve their reasons for unrest. I was still terribly uncomfortable about the definition of the third spirit.

Sometime later, maybe even years, I awakened one morning with what was to be the answer about the third, undefined spirit. The word "virtue" was as strong as it could be. Again, "virtue" was not a word I could associate with an evil spirit. It had the wrong connotation altogether. I spent much time analyzing this message but could not make it fit with a spirit at unrest. All of the messages I received were unfitting in my estimation. It wasn't making any sense to me at all.

ANGELS' EARTHLY CONFERENCE
ABOUT HOW A NEW STRUGGLE
SHOULD AFFECT MY LIFE

Angels in the Sky

CHAPTER FOURTEEN

Angels in the Sky

The alarm clock rang and I was awakened. I could feel that there were angels in the sky above me and they were having a discussion. What I saw in my mind's eye was this: angels or Gods, not in mystic form, but in human form, and wearing men's suits. They were facing one another as if around a table and in conference. They had emerged from a bed of clouds, as if they had broken through.

I stumbled out of bed and hit the snooze button on the alarm clock. I was aware of their existence, made my way back into bed, and went back to sleep.

The alarm rang some minutes later, and again I stumbled to the clock to turn it off, forcing myself to stay up so that I could get ready for work. I was still aware of the angels or Gods above, in conference. As I sat there pondering the presence of these angels, I decided to draw what I had seen.

I made my way to the kitchen to get a cup of coffee. I found a plain sheet of paper and then got a pencil from the kitchen drawer. I began to sketch.

What I learned by drawing was this. I had originally pictured these angels in the clouds in what appeared to be "boxes." I had thought that the box flaps had been turned outward. After I had drawn this vision, I realized that a break in the clouds had been made, like a tear in a sheet, which had made this folded-back look. I also realized that there were four male angels, and the one closest to the front, with his back to me, felt like it may have been my father. I was always feeling he was part of the many undefined spiritual revelations that I had.

I wondered what this conference was all about. I had hoped it had something to do with Steve, the man with whom I had dated and had become quite fond. Steve, like Matt, had found reason to leave my life. When the pressures of his divorce, change of business operation and dying mother became too great, he expressed a type of intermission would take place in the relationship and that we would date again in the Fall.

When I asked why the Gods were there, I received a karmic message. It had something to do with how a new struggle was to affect my life. I labeled the drawing as such. It did not say the struggle was related to Steve, but I did wonder. I had no idea what that struggle was to be.

CHAPTER FIFTEEN

A New Birth

I keep trying to see Gwenn's spiritual vision, as I see her floundering unhappily in her life. Still, there is no new spirit emerging from the rubble. Oh, wait, yes there is. There is a birthing process taking place.

A couple of weeks have gone by now, and the birthing process is still going on. What I see is that she will emerge as a new, whole person.

In talking to her today, I can tell she is not in good spirits. She is uncomfortable about her state in life and is unhappy. She is hoping this transition takes place quickly so that she can feel whole and go on with her life. She feels the "change" or metamorphosis that is going on.

CHAPTER SIXTEEN

Angel on the Way

I continued to worry about the people whose spiritual images I had taken on as a responsibility. A few nights ago, I checked Gwenn's vision to see where she was in the birthing process. To my alarm, she was almost reborn, but was dreadfully on fire. It was a vision I did not want to relate to her. However, I felt it was my responsibility to give her warning, if it indeed could help her in some way. I wanted to let her know.

I telephoned her but reached an answering machine. I left her a message saying, "What is going on? What I see does not look good."

When she returned the call, she explained what her week at work had been like. "It was just as you saw," she continued. "It was a week of people trying to 'burn' me at work."

A lady had written a threatening letter about her, and the secretary had bolded the scolding words and put them in capital letters. Gwenn's boss thought she owed the lady an apology, but Gwenn elected not to give her one. I was quite concerned about what I had seen, and was glad at the last check to see the fire almost out; she was charred, in part, but the smoldering of the ashes were all that was left of the fire.

Gwenn's rebirthing, at last glance, has almost been completed. And hovering in the air, on its way, is an angel coming to watch over her. She is not here yet, but is visible off in the distance. I was pleased to report that to Gwenn yesterday.

Today, Gwenn tried to reach me by telephone but I was not at home. She had spent two hours at work in a somewhat disoriented state. She felt this state had to do with a spiritual relationship. She was not tired and not stressed, but not quite able to make connectivity with her whole self. Something was going on. She was not alarmed by this, but was aware.

She called me in the evening to tell me she had wanted me to give her a reading this afternoon. She wondered if it had anything to do with the completion of her rebirth. Since I cannot always produce a vision on the spot, I agreed that I felt she was probably correct, and that I also felt that her angel had arrived. "I could sure use one, she said."

I asked her to think about whom this angel might me. I had thought it might be her late mother coming to watch over her. I explained that it was probably a family member that had passed on, or a very dear friend that she may have lost. She offered that she thought it might be her mother. The obscure part was that Gwenn had always been the one to take care of her mother, not her mother take care of her. I suggested that maybe now she was able to come to help, a way to repay, since she was not able to in her life's role as Gwenn's mother.

I agreed that I would try to take a good look at the angel's face when I could.

CHAPTER SEVENTEEN

Encounter of Precision

It was a pretty, sunny sort of day, and I was on my way to work. The traffic was clear, and I made my exit from the freeway as normal, and headed for the street where my place of work was located. In order to go west, I had to make a right turn going east and make my way to the left lane to the turnaround. I completed the turn, and there I sat, three cars back from the light.

To my left, approaching the same light from exactly the position from where I had just made my right-hand turn was Steve in his blue Mercedes. For that brief moment, the time it takes to stop traffic one way and allow for a clearing before the light turns green on the other side, I caught the glimpse of Steve's car, and looked inside to confirm that it was him.

At precisely the same time, with a one-to-two second delay, Steve recognized my car, and looked inside to confirm that it was me. He smiled his wide, gregarious smile with arms up and open in expression. I exchanged a warm smile and coy, small hand wave, with hand close to my body. Steve's greeting was one of welcomed surprise, but not unlike a greeting he would give to anyone he met up with by chance.

This meeting did not trigger a phone call from him, and I did not expect that it would. Therefore I did not set myself up for disappointment. The warm feeling of thoughts of him stayed with me for a couple of days, however, and I was again reminded of how strongly this man with musical interest literally brings music to my heart.

Steve may have been concerned this brief encounter might inspire a call from me, but it did not. I felt in my heart that Steve would call when he was ready, or something would happen to open the communication again and that is not now. I also felt very strongly that fate would work its hand, and that a number of brief encounters or a situation would occur that would bring a friendship back into play.

Just look at the precision that just took place. Steve and I had just traveled in traffic only a couple of minutes apart for the last twenty minutes. Knowing where he lived, I knew where he would have entered the freeway, and the timing was shortly after I passed his entrance ramp. He lived only ten minutes from me, and this in itself makes one wonder why a chance meeting does not occur more frequently.

It was not "planned" that we travel side-by-side in traffic. No, it was quite deliberate that we were to meet directly in view of one another without the distraction of traffic. This was planned as a place to meet face to face without the opportunity for verbal interaction, but with eye contact and a friendly exchange. It was then to be truncated by a changing traffic light.

No, this meeting was not by chance.

I later had dinner with Gwenn and discussed the events of my day, beginning with the awareness of the angels in the sky. I explained that I didn't see any relationship of the meeting of angels to my seeing Steve, but I really didn't know what it was about.

"What kind of discussion?" she asked, referring to the angels in the sky.

"I don't know. A conference," I said shrugging my shoulders.

"What was their mood?" she queried, still trying to get more out of this visual encounter.

"It was a calm discussion, a verbal exchange--a conference," I again offered.

"Maybe they were planning how you and Steve should have a chance meeting," she interjected.

"Maybe," I said. "I don't know if the events were related, but I definitely believe in fate. I believe firmly that fate had its hand in my seeing Steve, and it was only the first activity of the plan." There would be more to follow, I relayed.

"Oh, yes," said Gwenn. "Steve is not out of your life yet. There is a plan."

CHAPTER EIGHTEEN

Revisiting Old Ties

Life has brought about many changes. Most significantly is that fact that I have taken an early retirement from a job of 35 years, and at age 52 am trying out all of my learned skills in several part-time work endeavors. I'm finding that this age has brought about a new level of self confidence, and this new life, a taste of free spiritedness I have never before been able to enjoy. I need not be true or committed to any job, and have the option to skip around at will and try everything I find that I want to do.

As I sat and had a leisurely dinner with my friend and confidant, Gwenn, we exchanged much conversation about all of the events going on in our lives. We also reviewed mutually spiritual events of interest, such as my "visioning" ability and her gift to "interpret."

Over the course of the evening, she asked if I had looked at any visions recently, and I explained that I had not. No, I had not done much of that because of how full my life was at the time. I was not taking any time for that kind of concentration.

We visited a few visions together, recapping where we had left off on some, including hers, last seen after the completion of the rebirthing process. I explained that currently I saw her as her own person, but that she and the angel were quickly and alternately transformed--and that was constant. I had thought that the angel had come to watch over her, but now I wasn't so sure.

I did see Gwenn being neat and tidy, using her arms to straighten and put things away, and climbing very small mounds of dirt, like hills. She was making progress, I told her.

She then asked if I could see myself.

"Yes, I said. There is no change. I'm still on the hilltop, looking down over the world, in a white, flowing dress with a gentle breeze blowing my skirt."

"I see you as a butterfly," she said. "You are a beautiful butterfly, flitting freely from place to place."

"Oh, I said. Maybe you and I will not see the same spiritual image. Maybe we will be seeing different things."

"Maybe," she said.

It was not customary for Gwenn to see visions at all. It was her job to interpret. Now she was telling me of some things she could envision.

I then explained that I did feel enlightened about something. I felt that I was actually feeling that I knew things about myself from more than one past life. I began to relate the different visions and feelings that I had and how I counted four or five different lifetimes.

As we talked, we spoke about the life I had seen where I must have known the dark-skinned lady, and then another where there were galloping, white horses. Perhaps there was another where I knew of the gravesites of three buried persons. These were very vivid visions I had experienced. Others included standing outside a two-story apartment building at a road where there were no cars, and being in a sterile room which housed only a dead man on a cot.

She said, "I see you as a small child of about seven or eight years old. You are standing alone, watching, as the horses gallop by. I can feel the ground's vibration from the horse's hoofs. You have dark, straight hair, and are wearing a plain, straight, medium-colored brown dress.

"Like burlap?" I asked.

"I don't know," she said. "Just a medium shade of brown."

Her description caused me no consternation. It fit perfectly well with some visions I had seen. I agreed it was probably true.

CHAPTER NINETEEN

The Gods Haven't Decided

Several months later, I again awoke to the strong indication that the Gods were there and were back in conference. Steve had said we would date again in the Fall, but Fall came and there had been no call from him.

"He's not ready yet," said Gwenn.

It was now February. I trusted her judgement so thoroughly I agreed without question. I just assumed that we would reunite at some later time.

As the Gods conversed among themselves, I tried to listen to their conversation. Most was heard as a mere murmur and was not discernible. The feeling I got was that they had not decided if Steve and I should get back together again. They were discussing all of the aspects of each of our lives and were deciding if it was in each of our best interests to be brought back together again. In essence, at the end of their meeting, they had not decided. What they did decide, however, was that this was not the right time.

In the midst of my pain, I thought about the strong feelings I had for Steve and why I thought we would be good together. I also knew of the reasons why we would not, but was willing to work with them.

Steve was an extremely complex individual. While he did well to communicate his feelings in a humorous fashion, you really never knew where he was emotionally. He talked in riddles and codes, as one writer of zodiac signs related about Scorpios. It was the underlying motives, the deeply buried fears, and the well-hidden insecurities that needed to be understood to understand Steve.

I knew this and knew I would have to work hard on keeping these issues at the forefront of my mind. This would not be a natural course for me. I was too easily influenced by what I saw on the surface to remember to dig deeply for underlying definition. Even with this knowledge, I was willing to work on making a solid relationship. I would just wait until the Gods decided it was the right time. I just hoped they would decide it was right. I felt they would.

Many more months passed, and still no word from Steve. So much for my psychic ability, I thought. It felt so real. And, what about the Gods? Why had they been there? Why did they scheme so hard for that precision meeting of Steve and myself in traffic that one morning?

And why were they in conference in my presence? And again later, when they decided it was not a good time for us to reunite? I was puzzled. Why are they doing this to me? Don't they know how important he is to me?

I took note of a cartoon that appeared in a local paper prior to the anticipated year 2000. The first caption read "In Search of the Millennium." One definition I found of millennium was "a thousand years of peace."

Within the same cartoon, the next caption read, "Should Olde Acquaintance Be Forgot . . ." Steve's last name was Olde. How could such a message ever escape me! I now knew that we had a thousand years between our last lifetime and this, and I should not forget him.

CHAPTER TWENTY

True Accountings

Continuing our conversation over dinner one evening, I said to Gwenn, "I've been getting some messages lately, but I don't know what they mean."

"Like what?" she asked.

"First, recall the realization that my grandmother's spirit is a cat? And that costume jewelry pin of my mother's of a cat's head with those eerie emerald green eyes, so eerie that Matt turned it over in the box face down and put a rosary in with it before closing the cover? Well, just recently, on two different occasions, I have found emerald green stones in the house with no apparent reason. I have no idea where they are coming from."

With Gwenn's assistance, I later learned the emerald green cat eyes had come off of a tote bag she had made me and were not a psychic sign at all.

"And, remember when I was in trouble, and the Blessed Mother would squeak at me?" I continued. "Well, she had been silent for a very long time. She has recently squeaked at me a few times, but I'm not understanding the message."

The first time the series of squeaks began, I had placed the Blessed Mother statue in a box and kept her in my night stand. Gwenn had instructed me to take her out of the box and put her on my dresser. She explained that she wanted to help me, but needed to be where she could see me. I did as I was told.

"Anything else?" asked Gwenn.

"Yes, I said. You know how I've told you from time to time that someone would shake my bed in my sleep and would awaken me? And there never was anyone there, but I knew some spirit was responsible? Well, last night someone actually touched me personally. That is the first time that has ever happened. Three times during the night, someone shook my hand or my shoulder. No one was there that I could see, of course, but I'm sure I'm supposed to take note of something."

"What do you think?" Gwenn asked.

"I don't know," I said. "When someone shakes my bed, I usually think that may be my father, because Aunt Addie has spoken about someone shaking her bed, too. That would be her brother, you know. But this time I think it's my grandmother, but I don't know why. I just think it might be."

"What does she want?" asked Gwenn.

"I don't know, but I feel it must be some kind of warning, don't you?"

"Maybe."

As we were getting ready to leave, I expressed my concern to Gwenn about myself in that I felt that my new freedom was causing me to "run too fast" with all the excitement of the different things that I am now able to do with my life. I explained that I was running so fast that I was missing obvious things, passing streets because I was too far away in thought, and so on.

"That's your warning," she said. "Slow down! You're running too fast." That's the tap on the shoulder, the shaking of your hand or your arm. "Slow down!"

"You're probably right," I said. "That must be it."

"Read the paper when you go home tonight," she said.

"Why?" I asked.

"There's a message in there for you."

"A message," I asked? "I have to read the paper?" I moaned. "I hate reading the paper. This week's paper? Like the Sunday paper? Will it be on the front page?"

She shrugged her shoulders and put her arms up in question, as if to say I don't know where this is coming from. "What you're looking for has color in it."

"Like the real estate section?" I asked.

Again, with arms up in question, "There will be colored pictures on the page. That's all I know. Read the paper when you go home tonight."

We parted, and I drove home in the heavy rain. As I neared my street, I missed my turnoff. Recognizing this, and worrying that I knew I was still running too fast, I turned the car around and headed back toward my street.

I missed it again, found myself a little ways past my street going in the direction from where I had just come. I was frightened. I knew I had better concentrate on slowing down.

I finally made it home, and began talking to myself in slow motion to bring myself down. I moved slowly, decided to forego any mind-using activity for the evening and go directly to bed and relax. Unable to sleep, the second night in a row, I found myself tossing and turning. Again, finding myself awake until 3:00 a.m., I decided I would get up and look through the newspapers.

I went to the rack where I kept them. As I began to shuffle through discarded papers and ads, I came upon one which had colored pictures on the front page. I had looked at this paper previously without receiving any message. This time, at first glance, I picked up the paper and again read the headline, "Dr. R, Drop Dead." I knew it was meant for me. It was a warning to me to slow down or I would kill myself.

Dr. R was a local doctor who had taken it upon himself to assist terminally ill patients to end their lives. I threw the paper down, having gotten my message immediately. I smiled and went back to bed and to sleep.

The next morning I went back to look at the newspaper and noted the rest of the page. The second article also had a picture in color and was about the performance of some dangerous act. Something went wrong in the performance, but the actors had been rescued. It was just another warning of the risk in which I had placed myself.

This is a week later, and the Blessed Mother has not squeaked, and no one has visited me during my sleep.

CHAPTER TWENTY-ONE

The Pendulum Swings

One of the cutest things Rob did during his short stay in our lives was this. To give you the setting, Rob and Sue had just married and were temporarily living with me. Rob had bought a house for them, but it needed work prior to their moving in.

I was sitting in the kitchen one morning with elbows on the table, head propped in my hands, trying to wake up. Rob sleepily got up, made some small, annoying conversation on his way past me, and stumbled to the door to leave for work.

Suddenly, he came back through the kitchen, and I questioningly looked up at him with a puzzled expression on my face.

"Shoes," he replied. He had forgotten to put on his shoes!

That incident still brings laughter to my heart when I think of it. It was "so Rob."

Last evening, Sue was over, and we sat at the kitchen table doing invoicing and other work for our recently formed printing business. As she was getting ready to leave, we packed up the paperwork and other things accumulated in the house from the past couple of weeks' visits. I stood up and was prepared to help carry her things out to her car. She was on her way to the door, with me directly behind her, and stopped suddenly in the hallway. She then looked at me and said, "Shoes."

"Oh," I said. "You have the Rob curse."

"Yes, I do," she smiled. "But," as she walked back into the kitchen for her shoes, she said, "I don't have the old 'family curse' anymore." This was a quip from my perspective as the members of my former husband's side of the family were all overweight. Sue is still a little too heavy, but she must feel that she has it under control. That is a good sign.

She later explained that somewhere she had read an article in a magazine that explained the characteristics of a little-known eating disorder she felt she and other family members had. Just as an anorexic or bulimic person would look into a mirror and feel they were fat, she would look into the mirror and feel she looked thin, even though she was not.

Sue returned to the kitchen for her shoes, and spoke directly to the clock's pendulum saying, "Swing!" She was aware that it had not been working. It moved ever so slightly, with a nervous right-to-left movement.

I'm referring to a minuscule movement, but I said to her, "It looks like it wants to. I'll try it later." Rob's spirit must be ready to leave the house for a while and wants to let us know that, I thought. The "shoes" incident was the correlation needed to convey that message. Those subtle spirits were at work again.

I didn't try working with the pendulum until the following morning. I sat across from the clock while having my coffee, got up and pushed the pendulum behind the clock's glass face into a swinging motion. If it were not going to continue its movement it would have stopped within minutes, but it stayed in motion for twenty minutes. Its swing dwindled to a slower rate as the minutes passed. I could not remember what a normal swing motion should be for the clock's pendulum, and I continued to watch it slow its pace--but, "the pendulum does swing!"

I now took the clock off of the wall, cleaned its frame and glass, put new batteries in, even though it had been keeping exact time. I then placed it back on the wall. It has worked perfectly ever since. The pendulum swings.

My rationale is this. To keep their objectivity, spirits make sure there is some justification for their appearance. That is their way to keep hidden and for you never to be able to prove their existence. They are there, if you just watch for their signs, but they will stay transparent, mysterious and aloof.

CHAPTER TWENTY-TWO

Connected Souls

Now that I am not working, or at least the little work that I do is out of my home, I am in need of a fax machine. I occasionally impose on my good next-door neighbor, Kevin, to use his. While in his home office, waiting for my facsimile to go through, I saw paperwork on his desk of a recognized company name and familiar handwriting. It was Matt's, my former main man, and I can see that he and Kevin are still doing business together--but Kevin and I never discuss him.

I became entranced at the document, recognizing the perpetrator, and was unaware that Kevin was speaking to me. When I came around, he must have recognized the reason for my being lost in thought, but said nothing about it. What I felt was, as my friend Gwenn had told me many times, the connection of the souls.

Although I am too angry to entertain any thoughts of a compromised reunion between us ever again, and hold no current interest in that regard, I feel the connectivity very strongly and wonder how long that hold on me will last. He definitely made an impression on my life, but how long will it be with me? For the rest of my life? Until a suitable replacement for him is found? I wonder.

CHAPTER TWENTY-THREE

New Visions, Some Denied

I am still not working and do not have a routine built into my life. Nonetheless, my days are action packed and I have little idle time. With the busy life in which I find myself, I have not taken the time to take readings on all of the many persons with whom I can identify a spiritual image.

With most persons I can look at the symbolic image in my mind's eye and see what is going on with them at the present time. I can see if the person's life is in trouble, changing in some manner, or doing fine.

I've had to concentrate to bring forward a vision of a fairly close friend of a few years, now, for the first time. I never had a vision automatically enter my mind for her; I had to ask for it. Her name is Kristen, and she is the sweetest thing. I do know, however, that there is something underneath that has somehow been hurt deeply in her life. I believe the damage was done more in her upbringing than in her ended, hurtful marriage. That brought a level of devastation all of its own.

As a survival technique, she appears to have become, or maybe always was, selfish and self centered--but I must clarify--has no idea that she is and has no desire to exhibit these traits. She honestly does not understand that her actions are such, and truly means no harm to anyone. She is well worth the counsel to fix or modify these traits. I really believe it is a survival mode in which she has learned to live, as well as a resultant lack of self-confidence and self-worth that causes her to think and act in this way. I am not sure at what point it will be important to her to make changes to her life or to help her see these traits in herself.

It is clear to me that in the relationship she has with her children, that she has severely offended them all sometime in their lives. They have told her so in many words. She is constantly hurt by this and cannot understand how her current actions relate to what they are saying, what they feel, or why--because she just doesn't see it. There is absolutely no malice in her heart ever and she continues to be hurt.

In recent years, she has worked very hard to correct any prior wrongdoing with them, and has made more than ample effort to explain her past conduct. She has even acquired a mutual understanding with her children; however, after they give verbal forgiveness, they continue to revisit their hurt and replay the events of their pain to their mother. No amount of understanding, apology, or explanation has fixed this problem.

Her symbolic spiritual vision is portrayed to me as sweet dough, rolled in sugar. Gwenn's interpretation is that she is sweet on the surface because of the sugar coating. However, since the vision came with the definition of "sweet" dough, like a cookie dough, Gwenn quickly conceded and said, "It is not finished, then."

It was not until this writing that I thought to more clearly understand the visual image I received. Dough is either punched, rolled, kneaded, or otherwise pushed into form, and is perhaps mistreated in the construction of its final form. That might give an indication as to Kristen's earlier life. Despite all, she is truly as sweet inside as she is on the surface. That coating of sugar may be a trait added on later in life to deal with her fate.

Another spiritual vision appeared to me in regard to a new-found lady friend whom I recently met through Steve. She is a local musician and is legally blind. At the end of our first meeting, I went out of my way to exclaim to her from my heart that I found her to be an extraordinary woman. She completely impressed me with her ability to overlook her handicap and fully enjoy all that life had to offer—despite the hardships she would continue to encounter.

She has made several attempts to continue our friendship and has told me she immediately bonded with me as well. She also confided that with my ending comment to her the first evening we met, that she went into her house feeling like someone had just given her a bouquet of flowers.

Her spiritual vision came to me in reverse order. Normally I think of the person and the vision appears. With her, I was in my bedroom, glanced at my television's rabbit ears, and the image appeared. As my eye caught view of the antenna, I now saw many antennae and immediately thought of my new friend.

Demons in Blob Form

Of course, I mused, with her less-than-perfect sight she probably has antennae all over the place. She must use all of her senses more keenly than do others.

When we would get together, as a carryover from our first meeting, she continued to express an interest in reincarnation and my ability to see visual images. Much of our first discussions were on a spiritual level, and I was sure we would have many conversations in this regard in future meetings.

One evening, before retiring, I considered running through my list of persons I have neglected to reflect upon lately and see about their well being in my mind's "television."

With Lillian fresh on my mind, what I saw concerned me. What I should say is that the vision immensely disturbed me. I was virtually stunned. All I could see was a maze of demons in blob form and other unsightly characters. They had dark holes for eyes except for one. This one had my new friend's piercing, lighted eyes.

I haven't decided what this all means, but no matter who I tried to see of my close acquaintances, the appearance of this maze of characters thickened. Obviously, I had not called for THEM! I was still fully awake, but tired, and went to bed closing these visions out as I would turn off a television program I did not care to watch.

Were these visions telling me that all of life's hardships are caused by these demons that really do exist? Was it that "blob" with the piercing, lighted eyes that took my friend's sight?

As I consider this new vision, and especially the blob forms, I recalled Lillian had asked me if my visions contained real people or blobs. I told her "people or objects." I will have to ask her what she knows about blob forms. I have no idea how to tell her of what I have seen.

At my next meeting with her, I cautiously told her of the vision that I had seen. She did not seem to be alarmed, but in response exclaimed, "Everyone has a darker side, don't they?"

CHAPTER TWENTY-FOUR

A Scornful Woman

After a full day's activity, I had retired to my couch in front of my TV with a bag of freshly made popcorn. I watched the end of an exceptionally good movie, followed by another. My eyes started to close, and I forced myself to stay awake until the movie ended. Whatever followed was not particularly interesting, and I then drifted off to sleep.

When I awoke a short time later, a colorful silhouetted woman was in my vision, and was hanging right over my face. I was still in a laying position, and as I gazed up at her, she began to move backwards. She affixed herself to the center of my wall, and then moved up toward my ceiling. I did not know her, but I studied her intensely.

Only her head and body were manifested and rounded at the bottom. Her legs were not visible. She wore clothing, which was as transparent as was she.

I waited for something to happen, but nothing did. I was spellbound. I waited for her to move or to speak. She did neither. I was fully awake now, but in a trance staring at this woman. I couldn't believe what I was seeing and was caught frozen. I did not lift my gaze from her.

She was probably in her sixties. I was bothered that I did not know who she was. Her hair coloring was blond, and the same shade as my mother's had been, but it was not her. She wore a dark floral dress, and her complexion was Caucasian but vacant. Her expression, scornful. I believe I stared in awe of her for two to three minutes, not lifting my gaze, but she did not move. She had dropped her head to one side and stayed silent for some time. Suddenly, in an instant, she was gone.

I thought for a moment that perhaps she was my late mother, but I really didn't think so. I don't think I knew her. I felt that perhaps she was displeased about something or me because of the expression on her face. I wondered who she was and what she wanted. I turned the television volume off or down to where I could not hear it, and then concentrated my thoughts to that spot on the wall where she had been. I asked her who she was and what she wanted, but no vision reappeared. I then asked for a sign. I thought if I went back to watching television, perhaps I would get one, but I did not.

It is morning now, and I have awakened to reflect on the apparition I had seen. I was anxious to call Gwenn and tell her. When I did, Gwenn told me that she was not shocked that I had seen an apparition due to my ability to "see" things as I did anyway.

Gwenn tells me that if I do not know this woman, that I should not take her visit personally. It may be someone who had lived in my house years ago, or was just from this area. It may have nothing to do with me at all. I was just able to see her.

Gwenn later told me that she read that sometimes souls get lost when they are passing on, and find themselves in someone else's home. I may never know who this woman was, but I now feel she was just as perplexed as I and was trying to figure out who I was.

CHAPTER TWENTY-FIVE

Working Through Your Karma

Kristen and I have been friends for many years now. She is still that really sweet, dear person. You can always count on her to be honest about everything. She is what she is, and true to her word, like it or not.

What was not to like was that you could not always count on her to do things you planned with her, but her reasons were always honest and you could not deny that.

After a couple of disappointments, she began telling me right up front that she may not be doing what we plan when the time comes to do it, so don't make my plans around her. Her plans are always a plan, and they are not necessarily cast in stone. She makes sure that she wants to do the plan when the last hour is upon her.

She says, "I don't want to do things I don't want to do anymore. I'm tired of doing things because I think I should or I said I would."

That may be a good philosophy, but it leaves some, including myself, feeling she is selfish. She has not disappointed me in recent years, or else I've learned to accept that she reserves the right to change her mind and plan accordingly. I am more apt to think she has found our relationship of more value and has become more reliable.

Over the years that I have known her, the relationships she has with her children have somewhat mellowed as well. I'm not sure what their individual complaints had been, but they had seemed to relate better to their father on many occasions to Kristen's dismay. She is still terribly hurt from the divorce of more than twenty years ago. The reluctance on the part of her former husband to make any efforts of a friendship with her after all these years is still disconcerting.

After an evening's visitation with me at my daughter, Sue's, by Kristen and one of her daughters, I learned the next day how Rachel had relentlessly expounded on "their poor relationship." Hurting her deeply, Rachel made comparisons of their relationship to the relationship shared between my daughter and myself.

"I bet Sue's mother is always there for her," Rachel had said. "You can just tell she would do anything for her. You've never been there for me. In fact, you've never been there for any of us kids. Tara and Richard feel the same."

Those were very cutting words, and I felt very sorry for Kristen and for her children. "You don't make any effort with your grandchildren, either," Rachel continued. She was complaining that Kristen would never take any of her children for overnight stays, or even for a day's visit.

"I don't see why I can't have the same relationship with these children at your house as I would if I took them to mine," Kristen would try to reason. The underlying reasons for her reluctance were not understood. At first I didn't understand it either, but have later reasoned it may have to do with her self confidence more than not wanting to and may even go as deep as her feeling of self worth. It is certainly not because she does not want to spend the time with them.

When David was in her life, a man of significant respect, the two of them would keep two or three of the grandchildren overnight. Kristen was more than willing to do this with the added help. She must have felt more comfortable with his support.

In retrospect, she has admitted that in the earlier years of her divorced state, she was very unhappy and found it necessary to take care of her own emotional well being before the needs of her children. Her own fight for survival, which included personal male attention and entertainment would certainly make her children feel that preference as neglect. At one time or another in their adult life they have all railed at her about their relationships with her.

Her unhappiness stemmed from her husband leaving her for another woman and with small children to care for by herself. He also flaunted the other woman and made sure that the children had a relationship with the new woman after he married her. I know that was very painful for Kristen, and probably something I would not ever want to experience. She admits that her struggle sometimes caused her to take out her unhappiness on her children, and they have obviously never understood or been able to forgive her for it.

Additionally, family get-togethers for holidays or the grandchildren's birthdays are still difficult for Kristen due to her former husband's behavior. He goes out of his way to ignore her and generally be rude. He now has a third wife and even this has made no impact or change in his behavior.   He still makes these situations uncomfortable for Kristen and it bothers her immensely.

Time brings on many changes. Within the last six months, her son has been besieged with heartaches over a pending divorce of his own. Kristen claims that Richard was certainly a less-than-perfect husband, and was probably the cause of his own problems. Now that his marriage is at the end stage, he is now able to recognize his deficiencies and is more than willing to work on them to save the marriage.

Unfortunately, it appears that it is too late to save the marriage. As in most cases, when the difficulties are finally recognized, it is too late to correct them. His wife has a known boyfriend and there appears to be no reconciliation possible in the marriage in spite of Richard's courageous and continuing efforts.

Now, after all of the years of despising his mother for her apparent weak and unwarranted actions with him during his childhood, he finally realizes how the shoe fits. He is now forced to see his small children's family life threatened and feels the devastation and loss of his wife's love and affection. He now calls upon Kristen frequently for her guidance and support, and depends heavily on her friendship.

"You know, Mom, I guess I can tell you now. For years I hated you. I thought you were a terrible Mom. Now I can see what you were faced with."

After much counseling with her son about his mistakes and how to get a grip on his current situation, he has come to appreciate her. I personally feel she has given him excellent support and advice.

With his statement, she asked, "And how do you feel about me now?"

"I think you're great," said Richard. "I think you're a wonderful Mom, and I really appreciate how much you have helped me."

Just previous to this, one of Kristen's daughters, Rachel, also had a small reconciliation with her Mom. They had a heart-to-heart talk, as they had many times before, which usually ended in disaster. This time, however, it was different.

A friend of Rachel's had said some things that finally made an impression with her. She had related how difficult it must have been for her Mom all of those years struggling to keep their home together with their father off doing his own thing. She pointed out that her father had given up his part of the responsibility to take care of them. She also told her how good it was of her Mom to be able to keep that home for them, despite how arduous and emotionally agonizing it must have been for her.

Rachel related this to Kristen, now, as if to say she had failed to understand her Mom's position all of these years.

Upon returning home one evening, I sat in my driveway still in Kristen's car. We had been talking about a recent family function she had attended at one of her daughter's houses that past weekend. Her ex-husband, as usual, had been a jerk in her estimation, still refusing to be civil with her.

"I told Tara to tell her father that he doesn't need to worry about me wanting him anymore. I wouldn't have him now if he were available to me," she said.

"Oh?" I responded. Whirling thoughts circled in my head.

"That's what Tara told me," she said. "My daughter told me that she had talked with her dad about his treatment of me, and his comment was that he didn't talk to me because he didn't want to give me any false hope. Can you believe that?"

"No," I said.

"Well, I can honestly say for the first time in my life that I don't want him. After all these years I can finally see through him, and I don't want him any more."

"Kristen," I said, "that's wonderful. Do you realize that you are finally working through your karma? You have reconciled with your daughter, Rachel, then Richard, and now your relationship with your ex-husband. This has all happened in a very short time, like within the last six months. You now only have to resolve the difficulties between you and Tara, and you will have completed your karma."

"I hadn't given it any thought," she said. "Thanks for listening."

CHAPTER TWENTY-SIX

Oh, the Pain in My Heart

Meeting Russ was certainly an uplifting experience, even if he never called me. It just felt good to know that someone could be so enticing, so intriguing, and so captivating as to steal your heart upon the first meeting. Of course, I knew it would probably never be a good relationship anyway, but oh, so delightfully enchanting.

I hoped I would by chance see him again, perhaps at By-the-Bay where we met. At the same time I knew it would be trouble. Russ had been completely fortified with alcohol the night I met him. A red flag goes up immediately with me whenever anyone orders a double anything. He was just so complimentary and exciting that it would have been difficult to not be enamored with him.

He had called me late that same evening, after I had returned home, which made me feel that he was just as enamored with me. However, I am sure he lost my phone number that night in his drunken state. Gratefully, taking my best interests into consideration, I never heard from him again.

I was not dating anyone meaningful at the present time. I had surgery a week or so after having met Russ, and now I was recovering. I had not been anywhere for the last month, and was not doing a whole lot of anything socially. I was more apt to spend my social time with girlfriends and to catch up on what was going on with them.

I had been getting calls from Lillian for the past two weeks. She, coincidentally, had a similar surgery the week prior to mine. I was unable to meet with her last weekend due to other obligations, but agreed to see her Friday evening after work for dinner.

I picked her up and we went to a relatively new and busy restaurant on her side of town. It just so happened that we both knew the owner for different reasons, and I was very surprised to learn of his third successful restaurant on the east side of town.

Lillian and I shared a lot of conversation about many things, and occasionally about our current male acquaintances. She had been seeing a man for a long time who recently married someone despite their ongoing relationship. He had insisted that she attend his wedding and after formally declining, she had reluctantly agreed to go.

She had confided in me about the wedding and about her male friend. His intentions were to continue to see her, but she felt she would not want to see him again. After all, he had made his choice.

Steve and I stopped going out shortly after Lillian and I met. I knew when he backed away from the relationship that there was nothing wrong between he and I and that it was due to the burdensome circumstances currently in his life.

I was extremely disappointed to lose him and missed dating him terribly. I had hoped when things settled down for him he would return in my life as he said he would.

Because he was her friend as well, Lillian asked that we not discuss Steve as it put her in an uncomfortable position. I understood and agreed, but wished I could learn some inside information about him. I obliged, and never asked about him. She would occasionally mention his name, or say how well he had spoken of me, but I never asked for more information than she was willing to offer.

After a few months of pain, the newly-wed gentleman made his way back into Lillian's heart and bed and the relationship continued as an affair rather than the relationship it had once been. She wished she would meet someone just as captivating so she could let go of him, but that had not happened. It probably could not happen while she was so emotionally involved with him.

I had no idea how she was enduring the pain she was experiencing. I, of course, have kept her secret, and have never relayed this information to anyone. I did not even tell Steve who is one of her musical students. Steve may have picked up on this himself but was too much of a gentleman to ever say.

This particular evening's conversation brushed on the fact that we both needed to meet someone new, and I agreed that would be nice. I then relayed the information about having just met the most exciting man, but that I knew he would not be good for me.

"Most exciting?" she asked knowing how I had felt about her friend and piano student, Steve.

"Yes, most exciting! Nothing came of it, but he was truly the most exciting man I have ever met. He called himself impetuous, and he certainly was."

"They call that A.D.D. (Attention Deficit Disorder), she quipped."

"Yes," I agreed. "He probably was." In fact, he was probably more 'manic' than Matt was, which may have accounted for some of the attraction. I always seemed to attract the free-spirited, and a little-bit-crazy type of personality. It complimented my quietness, and allowed me to follow comfortably where I would not venture on my own.

On the other hand, there have been some males that I have been with who repressed my spontaneity and the ability to express my limited free spiritedness. I would feel like I was in chains.

"How long did you go with Matt?" she asked, as she had not known me during that time.

"For fourteen years," I replied. "It was just like a marriage that never happened."

"That must have gone on while you were still married, then," she questioningly stated.

"It did. My marriage was virtually over, but we began as co-worker friends. My divorce took five filings and nine years before we completed it."

"Wow. That's a record!" Lillian said. "You deserve an honor."

"He was married, too, but his marriage went on longer than mine. He had three boys, but the last one was still very young. I'm sure that had a lot to do with his hanging on to the marriage so long. When he did leave the marriage, he was already making plans to leave me too, and he did."

"Everything but the papers," she said. "I have my own feelings about that. It was a marriage just the same."

"Yes, it really was. He left because he didn't want another marriage so soon, and felt obligated because of our long-term relationship. Then I met Steve!"

"Oh, she said. How unfortunate for you," knowing that Steve left me.

"Well," I said, secretly feeling that Steve would appear in my life again someday, "I have to say that Steve got me past Matt nicely because I cared about him so much."

"Yes, the replacement theory always works," she offered, "and you recognized a good man when you found one."

"I will tell you honestly that I didn't actually get over

Steve until the night I met Russ. Even though nothing became of it, it was great to be enamored by someone. He was so complimentary towards me it was enough to take my mind off of Steve."

"Oh," she said, "then I can tell you--enough time has passed anyway."

"Tell me what?" I questioned, dreading what I was about to hear."

Since Lillian is legally blind, she was unable to read my alarmed facial expression. She sensed my silence and said, "Are you sure?"

Knowing I had to hear this, and hiding my apprehension as best as I could, I said "Yes."

"Steve has been seeing someone now for quite a while, and it looks very serious."

"Oh," I said, despair striking my heart.

"Darlene was introduced to him by someone, and they seemed to hit it off very well. I hear she is a lovely girl."

"I'm sure she is," knowing that Steve would not be with someone who was not.

In this conversation I learned that Lillian and Steve talk occasionally, but not often. He is no longer taking piano lessons from her. She said he is just too busy with his newly moved practice, which I knew about.

"Whenever we talk, we both laugh," she said. "You know how he is. But he doesn't want to get married," she added.

Thank God, I thought! This was enough pain for me to endure.

"I wouldn't be surprised if this relationship isn't a rebound from his marriage," I offered.

"Oh, I don't think so. I really think he's serious about her. That divorce started a long time ago, maybe four years ago now."

"I know."

"Unfortunately, I think you were the first girl he dated."

"Yes, I think I was too. I know he dated a couple of times before me, but not steadily, and probably just once or twice.

Sensing that this discussion hurt me Lillian said, "I think I shouldn't have told you. This wasn't meant to hurt you."

"That's okay, I said. To be honest, it does hurt, but I would have to know. You know that."

"Yes, I suppose you would."

"When did he meet her?" I asked.

"Well, what year is this? '98? It must have been the Fall of '96," she said. "August of '96."

I had dated Steve until June of '96. He had planned to date me again, and look what happened, I thought. Someone introduced this girl to him and he really liked her. My heart was aching.

Again Lillian said, "I'm sorry this hurt you. That was not the intent."

"I know. It is better that I know, though," I said.

"I suppose it is."

Fate had been kind, I thought. I had not run into Steve with this woman. That would have been extremely painful. Now it would be painful even if he were by himself, as I would know.

"How is your British friend?" asked Lillian. "I don't remember his name. Are you still seeing him?"

"Oh, yes," I said. "What is his name?" I jokingly stammered. I had sudden memory loss, still absorbed in thoughts of Steve.

"I can tell how important he is to you," mused Lillian.

"Yes, can't you tell? His name is Duncan. I saw him a couple of weeks ago. In fact, we went to Canada and had dinner at a British Pub, the same one Steve and I stopped at on the way home from his cottage."

"Oh, you went to Steve's cottage with him?" Lillian was considering the closeness of my relationship with Steve.

"Yes. In fact, I probably never told you, but when I was a small child, my mother and dad had taken me on a vacation with my aunt, uncle and cousin with whom I had been raised. We went to a cottage in Canada at this same resort. When I went to Steve's cottage, I really looked it over to see if it may have been the same one."

"You mean you may have stayed in Steve's cottage when you were younger?"

"I might have, but I really can't be sure. If not, and it probably was not, it was certainly very close to there. The scenery and surroundings were too familiar. I studied the kitchen, because that is what I remembered, but it didn't seem like the same one. The cottage I had been in had a larger kitchen, I thought. But, other furniture or another arrangement of furniture could certainly make it look different, and I was a young child."

Lillian took in the information as I continued.

"The interesting part is that I remember my uncle playing a guitar that had been in the cottage, and Steve told me his father always had instruments around. We also talked about a trick glass that was found in the cupboard and a 'whoopee cushion' that was left under a cushion of one of the chairs. The glass had slits for liquids to leak out and drip on the user's chin, and the 'whoopee cushion' made an embarrassing noise when you sat down in the chair. Steve had said that both of those items had been in the cottage at one time, but many of the neighbors had enjoyed practical jokes. That may not be a positive indication."

It would be just too fateful if this were the same cottage I had stayed in as a child.

CHAPTER TWENTY-SEVEN

That Mean Family Spirit

It was as if an exorcism needed to be performed. If I could have seen my daughter in person rather than the telephone conversation we were having, I'm sure I would have seen her head spinning in complete circles.

She had been going to school at night and working full time, and it was getting close to exam time. Stress was mounting and the pressure was on. She also needed to register for the next semester at school, and had casually mentioned that she didn't know how she was going to pay for it.

I knew my daughter well enough to know that she hadn't saved a dime toward the next semester's tuition. That was not her nature. She spent money freely and her habit was to live lavishly. If there was enough money left over, she would then pay the bills. For this reason, I was never too quick to offer to pay for things about which I thought she should be more responsible.

She had applied for school loans from time to time, and if she needed money for school, she would always ask. I would accommodate her with a loan, and she always would pay back the money she had borrowed. The pay back was never by making payments, however. It was because she had acquired a lump sum of money, and knowing she owed the money would pay up.

I do have to give her credit for this much responsibility. I allowed her to pay off all of her debts with me, which were sizable, so that she could feel good about the responsibility of repayment. I always intended to financially reward her for this by a gift toward school tuition, but the mode had been set to make her responsible for herself. I neglected to offer. I had completely forgotten my intentions.

She was working for her brother at his business and had somehow worked out with the accountant that her school loan be paid for by the company. So, I wasn't too concerned with her tuition money at the time. This situation was taking advantage of her brother, I knew, but if he wasn't man enough to step in, so be it. It was for a good cause.

Her recent conversations had been how she would like to quit work all together and go to school full time. This is a girl who is approaching 30 years of age, and I personally didn't feel she needed to be supported at her age so that she could just go to school. I felt it was her "not wanting to take responsibility for herself" behind her motivation, and I was unwilling to give her any encouragement in this area. I went to school full time, worked full time, raised a family and kept up a house. It was difficult, but I managed.

She had been exceptionally emotional lately with the pressures of finals, planning for graduate school, and with a boyfriend who was seemingly or suspected to be unfaithful. This had not been proven, but was of great concern to her. I found his disposition to be rather terse anyway, as she of course relayed the bad parts of their relationship. I was not fond of him for her from the things that I had learned, but heaven knows sometimes I felt they deserved one another. I later learned to understand his disposition better and see his warmer side.

Sue had been to a graduate school planning seminar to find that her grades had probably not been quite as high as she needed, or that they were borderline enough as to not give her any room for even a small failure. This was to add more pressure to her already stressed-out state. She explained that she was formulating a plan, and when she was ready, she would like to discuss it with me. I said that would be fine.

She had complained steadily about her drive from work to school, and how it was too far. I drove that far three nights a week to her two when I was getting my degree. I somehow felt that the complaint about the drive was a motivation to live closer to Norm. He was not pleased with driving to the east side of town. He many times commented on it being too far to drive to her place. I felt she was too willing to accommodate him.

Sue complained that she couldn't keep up with cleaning her condo and doing her washing. It was just too much with going to school. I cleaned a house four times the size of her condo and cooked and washed for a family of four. I couldn't understand why she thought her life had to be so easy. You had to work hard for what you wanted!

"Dad probably helped you with the cleaning and cooking," she said.

"No, he didn't," I remarked, "but he did stay home with you kids at night which allowed me to go to school. I couldn't have done it without him. But I did the rest by myself, without complaint."

I could appreciate how tired she felt. I remembered that part well. The difference was that I just took it in stride as part of the program; it didn't occur to me to complain or to ask my husband to support me so that I could go to school full time. I could not comprehend the feelings she had that her life was too difficult.

She was now ready to discuss her plan. It was to be a manipulative plan, I soon learned. Her conversation began with, "How would you like to make an investment in my education?"

Well, of course, how could a mother say "no" to that?

"What have you got in mind, honey?" I asked.

"Well, you know that $10,000 you loaned me to buy my condo? I want to sell the condo and use the money to go to school full time."

"Where would you live, then?" I asked. I already knew she had inquired about living on campus and had been denied. She was too old and did not have a child to raise on her own, thankfully, which would have qualified her.

"I could rent something closer to school," she said.

Well, I knew that renting would cost her more money than what she was paying for her condo and the maintenance fee put together, and it just didn't seem wise to me. I certainly didn't feel comfortable about taking $10,000 and just watching it fall through her fingers. I couldn't see her being able to hang on to the money so that it would be available for school when she needed it, and if she didn't plan to work, where was the money for rent going to come from?

"No, I can't agree to that," I said.

Enraged that her well-calculated plan did not work, she said, "You have the money. If you're not willing to help me, don't expect any help from me. I'll do what I want anyway. I'll sell the place, give you your money, and then we don't have to talk any more!"

"You can do that if you want to," I calmly responded. "I never said I wouldn't help you; I just can't agree with your logic."

"It's a parent's obligation to put their children through school," the wicked voice continued. "I thought you'd be proud of me for going to school, and I've proven to you that I can do that. I don't know why you don't want to help me."

"I am proud of you for going to school. Very proud. But it isn't my obligation to put you through school. I haven't seen you save any money towards school, and I don't believe in free rides. I don't know why you feel you shouldn't have to work. You've always had a problem with responsibility, and I think that you just don't want to be responsible for yourself."

She didn't respond to my statements. To have her not retaliate was quite surprising to me in her current state of mind. She undoubtedly knew I was correct in what I had said.

"I never said I wouldn't help you. I just haven't seen you do anything to prepare for paying for your classes."

Again, no comment. She knew that I was right.

"I'm glad that you are going to school, but I think you should be able to work and go to school."

"You just want to control me," that meanness continued. "You've always wanted to control me."

"I'm just trying to guide you. I am always there to help you, but I'm not going to do it for you. You have to work on paying for your education too."

"Well, Norm's mom said I could live with her, and Norm said he would pay for me to go to school," she hatefully continued.

"You can do that if you want to," I said, "but I don't think you would want to." I knew that even though her ultimate plan was to force herself upon Norm so that he wouldn't get away, even she couldn't compromise herself that much.

"Well, can I come back and live with you?" she asked, knowing full well she wouldn't want to do that at all.

"Yes. I suppose you can, but I doubt you'd want to give up your independence to do that, would you?" I was already mentally formulating how bad our relationship would become if we were to be under one roof and I had to put up with Norm. I wasn't sure at that point that I liked him. I certainly wouldn't want him to spend the weekends with me in my home and take up my living room space! I would lose all of my privacy in my own home. How dreadful a thought.

The conversation ended on an inferior note and barely tolerable. I felt terrible for the friction between us, and hoped that I had said the right things. The next couple of days were testy. I decided to ignore the fact that we had any confrontation or uncomfortable words. I continued to call her for small conversation, being careful not to ask her for anything that she might misconstrue as "help."

I thought about that mean family spirit that lurked within our lineage. It had carried itself from my grandmother to my mother, to myself, and now, clearly to my daughter, Sue. What was that mean spirit all about? Why could it not rest? What did it want, anyway? I didn't know.

By the third day Sue seemed to simmer down. At one point she actually called me for something. I reacted mildly, as if I hadn't noticed the change, and we somehow made plans to have dinner. With her improved attitude and acceptance of my stern feelings, I got out the checkbook and wrote a check to cover her next semester at school.

It was then that I realized that I had meant to reward her earlier for her diligence in paying back all loans. I felt the check was generous enough at this point in time, but that it would keep things in check so that she would still have to learn "responsibility." That is, I am quite sure, what her mission in life is to be. She is here to learn "responsibility," and I feared she may not learn it in this lifetime. Recent years have shown a more responsible girl. I'm quite pleased with her progress.

She was more than pleased with the check. It seemed to relieve much of the pressure that she was feeling. I now think she was probably feeling displeased with herself and incompetent for not having done her part in saving for school. She was up against a brick wall with no place to go. She was also standing on loose ground where Norm was concerned, and that was not comfortable either. I was there to catch her wrath, because I was the only one with whom she could vent. She also felt that I had let her down.

The following week we went to dinner again, at her suggestion. This time she had a small gift for me. It was a crocheted vest that she had purchased when she was in Florida visiting her dad. She wanted me to have it then, along with a cute little card apologizing for her behavior. The card basically said, "When I was at the end of my rope, you were there. Then I realized you were there for me all along."

That was the daughter I knew. She was appreciative of the care and love I had for her. That mean spirit appears to be within an entire female family line. Regretfully I can admit to its surfacing within me.

When under extreme pressure, the dragon's tongue emerges, the head spins, and the whole world is wrong. The expression of "seeing red" is unparalleled. Something takes over, and the mouth becomes out of control. The mind searches for the most cutting words to voice and that will do the most damage.

Matt used to call me 'Lucy,' which he said was short for Lucifer, when this would happen--which was during the period of my emanating divorce. Fortunately, that ruthless spirit has been calmed within my soul.

I only hope that its ugly match, contained within Norm's soul, will not attach itself permanently within my daughter's heart. I have seen an internal anger, directed toward himself, but which is apt to overflow. That would only propagate the viciousness like a disease. A man with a kind and sensitive nature could calm the wrath that unhealthily lurks within her being. The kind soul of Matt settled my barbaric spirit, and may it continue to rest in peace within me.

It is strange how fate works. While Sue was making her plans, her brother was at a point in his business to have to cut costs. Even though he loved his sister and allowed her to take advantage of the business for some time, he now was being pushed into having to lay her off. He told me it was the most difficult decision he has ever had to make in his life. He regretted having to do it. He has a heart of gold, and it was very painful for him.

On the plus side, that is exactly what Sue wanted to have happen. That allowed her to collect unemployment and register for school full time. The timing was perfect for her purposes.

She then went to the Veteran's Administration office and reapplied for her V.A. pension, to which she was entitled as long as she did not work. The pension was earned through her short marriage to Rob, and one which she had previously collected upon his sudden death.

Upon going to the unemployment office, she was told that her obligation to look for work would be waived as long as she was a full-time student. She could collect for twenty-six weeks, which would get her through half a year, and then apply for an extension.

It is strange how things work out, isn't it?

CHAPTER TWENTY-EIGHT

Debt Paid

I was talking to my daughter, Sue, who asked me about her spiritual image and what I had seen lately. I told her that I still saw the tree-like trunk around her. It had opened up and had given her wide berth to walk in and out freely, but it had not released her. I had always felt that some evil spirit had been keeping her confined and had been putting strife into her life. The tree-like trunk was not really made of bark, however, but a wet substance.

"Maybe it will by my 26th birthday," she said, and she reminded me that she could not ever see her life beyond age 25. In fact, it was very important to her that she be married and have a child by that age for that very reason. She never did have a child, however. By her own choice she elected to end the pregnancy. It was not because she did not experience the ability to get pregnant. It was just the unfortunate circumstances around Rob's death that caused her to make that decision.

After we spoke, I decided to take a reading of her spiritual vision. She was not in the trunk of that tree-like substance at all. If fact, although I could not tell you of any object within that tree, I felt as though she and her belongings had vacated the premises.

I asked where she was, and saw something hovering

above the jagged top of the tree trunk. At first I thought whatever I was seeing was somewhat angelic, as I saw sheer, delicate wings. Then I saw a long, pointed beak, like that of a humming bird. It was difficult to bring the vision in. I left it alone for a while and then came back to it later.

It was a humming bird, and it was not entirely free to go. It appeared to have a single thread holding it there and it could not leave. I could see that it was happy, however.

I looked up humming bird in the dictionary to confirm it was the likeness of what I had seen. It was, and it was defined as a New World bird. Perhaps Sue is almost ready to enter a new world, one without the reincarnated soul sharing her body with her own soul as it had. At least that is what one psychic I had seen had explained. She had said Sue would not find peace until she found the common thread that would unite her current life with the soul of her past. I could now see that thread.

Gwenn suggested that her reincarnated soul and Rob's previous life's soul had some unfinished business to take care of, and that Sue and Rob were never supposed to share a lifetime together. Their short two-year relationship and four-month marriage was only a means to finish out something left undone in a previous lifetime. She thought that perhaps they each had a debt to pay.

I asked her to expand on that. She explained, with speculation, that perhaps in Rob's previous life he had brought pain or death to someone unnecessarily or unscrupulously. It may have been some encounter with

Sue's reincarnated soul. He was tormented his entire time in this lifetime because he had a debt to pay for the suffering that he had caused in a previous life. Thus, he ended his own life in payment of his debt.

This was an interesting concept to ponder, I had to admit.

"And Sue's purpose for this pain?" I asked. "Maybe she caused pain to others in a previous lifetime and it was now her turn to feel a loss," Gwenn said.

CHAPTER TWENTY-NINE

Burn Spirits, Burn

I was on vacation with Mike, my latest love. It was a love that had a specific purpose for us each to accomplish. The love had been dwindling in recent months, and I was not ecstatic about this vacation in the first place. I spent every evening reading a good book before actually retiring for the night. Mike went to sleep soon after getting into bed, so it did not seem uncomfortable that I read for a while.

On one particular night I had read all I wanted, but still was not tired enough to go right to sleep. I got into bed, but let my thoughts drift. I usually amused myself checking on the people I watched over by viewing their symbolic mental images that I had conceived of them.

My daughter's tree-like stump appeared. That was the symbolic image I had received as to her place in life. I had not asked for it. It was burning. It was fire-red and burning. Next, my mother's dragon appeared from behind the tree stump. It, too, had caught on fire. It's head thrashed in an effort to rid itself of the fire, but it had already been overly consumed by the blaze. I watched with complete astonishment, wondering what this all meant. I knew it had some real significance, but didn't have a clue as to what it was.

The dragon was fighting death quite diligently. Its head and upper body wavered from side to side as it tried to escape the burning. By now the fire had reached its

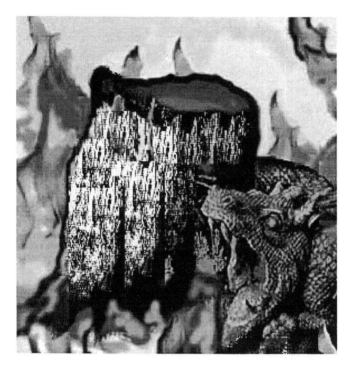

Burn Spirits, Burn

head, and the dragon was still fighting. Now a close-up view of the dragon's head presented itself. It was a captioned view resembling the movements of the well-known lion of a movie production house.

It was the dragon's last effort to withhold its inner substance, but all was expelled as it fought fervently to stay alive. At last, its mouth opened wide, as if to disgorge the last of its life. The word "divulged" came through as a psychic message. Its entire inner being had been laid open, exposed and revealed.

I stared through my mind's eye. What did this all mean? The tree stump had died. It had been killed off. The dragon fought so hard, it was difficult to see if it had been completely finished off, but I believe it was. It did not want to die, and in the end it had divulged all.

I read something sent to me in an e-mail around Halloween which was to be a list of rules to follow. Two of them struck me as being appropriate, so I repeat them here. The author is unknown.

> 1. When it appears that you have killed the monster, NEVER check to see if it's really dead.

> 2. Never read a book of demon summoning aloud, even as a joke.

This seemed to me to be a good practice, indeed.

I knew I must consult with Gwenn. She is the only one who can explain to me what really happened. She is my psychic interpreter of the visions that I have. We met for dinner, as we often did.

After the events of the week had been exchanged and our dinners consumed, we then sat face to face and communicated the karmic happenings of our lives. We assessed where we each were in the spiritual world, and considered the other characters in our massive "playground." I explained to her of the burning of these two very important spirits in my life. I had hoped that she could offer some valid explanation.

These were two very crucial events of my mind's picturesque movie screen. I explained the occurrences just as I had seen them, asking her what she thought they meant.

"And what did it mean for them to burn together?" I asked. "You know, Sue always did feel a closeness with my mother. Despite the fact that she spent little time with my children, Sue well remembers those cherished memories with fond affection for her."

"There probably is some connection, but I don't know what it is," Gwenn responded. I'd say the tree stump represents a turning point in Sue's life. You may not see any difference in her, but there will be changes. She may take on more responsibility for her own life now. She may start looking out for herself more."

"I was hoping I'd see a change in her disposition, but I haven't. You know she needs to wake up in regard to Norm. She seems unhappy but won't admit it to herself. She is so frustrated by him."

"That won't come so quickly, as she is still struggling with who she is. Subconsciously she is figuring out what it is that she needs, whether or not it is apparent in her conscious mind."

"You're probably right," I said, "and I'm glad to report that my son is finally coming around, too. Every time I talk to him and ask him what he's doing, he tells me he is looking out for himself."

"He's sure growing up in a hurry, isn't he," Gwenn exclaimed. She knew of the struggles he has had trying to save his father's poorly managed and disreputable business.

His father had given up and had gone to Florida to live. I knew his intentions were good and that he meant to leave his son with a thriving business. Instead he left him with a debt of unpaid taxes, one from which he could not recover. Doug had filed Chapter 11, hired both an attorney and an accountant that acted as consultants, and tried for months to pull the business out of its devastating state.

Just this week, after many times stating "the business is going to have to close," he surrendered a voluntary Chapter Seven bankruptcy. There was no way he could recover from many years of accumulated debt.

George, his salesman, has been like a father to him. In fact, he has been a father to both of my children in many ways. Sue borrowed a large sum of money from him to get herself out of debt, which was a normal occurrence if you followed her history. She was too embarrassed to come to me again. She really is trying to redeem herself with independence and taking responsibility for her own errors. I give her much credit for this. She knows what is right and takes it upon herself to correct it. I'm really quite proud of both of my children. They've made mistakes as we all do, but are both very bright in their own independent ways.

Doug, Sue tells me, has had his eyes opened in regard to his father's capabilities versus his own lately. She tells me that Doug is finally realizing that his father isn't the all-perfect person he has held in high esteem for such a long time. His father is human and makes mistakes too.

While he naturally believed his father was all-knowing and always right, he is beginning to understand that his well-taught non-reputable tactics were not always sound. I have tried to tell him that his father had paid dearly for many of his shrewd business antics. I think he is beginning to understand, although the quick mind, like his father's, is so tempted to outsmart normal channels.

Now, the burning of the dragon had to be discussed. "Why did the dragon burn along with the tree stump?" I asked Gwenn. We discussed various aspects of this scene, but I still wasn't getting an answer I wanted.

Like all other psychic offerings from Gwenn, when it entered her mind, she would speak from somewhere within. It was never a carefully thought out process, but an immediate, knowing response.

"Your mother is going to be reborn," she said.

I was immediately in tune with this informative exclamation. "That means someone in my family is going to give birth soon," I said. Doug and Janelle will probably have a baby."

My son and his live-in girlfriend are to be married this coming August, and Doug had told me how much Janelle wants to have another child. Her boy, Donald, is seven years old now, and she has wanted another baby for some time.

"It might not be your immediate family, you know," continued Gwenn. "It might be a child born in your cousin's family."

"Yes, I know. That thought had already gone through my mind."

"When you look at the baby's face, you will know," she said.

"Oh, I'm sorry for the troubled soul that will again need to be dealt with."

"She will be born again, but without those demons that her last husband had referred to. She will be free of them. That is why the 'burning' took place. Burning is a purification, a cleansing. They will be gone."

"I sure hope so. What a troubled soul that would be." I knew how terribly chaotic and disturbed my mother's life and behavior had been by them.

So that's it, I thought. My mother is to be reborn. The reincarnation process is at work.

Gwenn and I were engulfed in our private conversation. I momentarily stepped out of our world and looked around me. "You know, the people sitting around us haven't a clue as to what is really going on in this world. If they overheard our conversation, they would think we were really insane." It amused me.

"I know," said Gwenn. "It all depends at what level they are in spiritual development. We just happen to understand because we have reached that level of awareness."

"I'm sure you're right."

A couple of days later, I thought about the burning of the two symbolic spirits and Gwenn's comment about a turning point in Sue's life. I decided to take a look at each of my family's symbolic forms for any changes I could see. I also thought about the third, undefined spirit. This is what I found.

> My former husband's symbolic form had been of a serpent in the water—now I was seeing a drowning man.
>
> My son's image had been a water snake—he now has been put out to dry, but in the next scene is standing tall. He looks boxy, not upright and is leaning back. I would say he hasn't quite 'straightened' his life out yet, but it looks like he will. The water snake is

obviously going away. Being 'put-out-to-dry' does relate to the closed business venture belonging to him and his father.

My daughter, formerly seen as confined in a tree stump—is now standing tall, but is not as tall as her brother. She is also seen as boxy and leaning slightly back.

As for me, formerly viewed as a woman standing on top of a hill overlooking all that I can see—I'm no longer just standing there; I'm walking across the meadow.

I asked Gwenn what it meant to be "boxy," and she said sturdy, and with squared shoulders. I tried to put some of the pieces together. I can only assume that it is a time of renewal for us all.

Now a "vision" of the third, unidentified spirit was coming through as an answer to my request. I cannot make any sense out of it, but I know it is in relation to the third spirit. I can only describe it by effect. It is a "sucking in." I see pursed lips, strenuously sucking in, and really working hard at it. I cannot describe it any differently or name it appropriately. I just know it represents the third spirit. Something or someone has been sucked in.

I knew I would have to present this information to Gwenn for some insight. I hoped that she would be able to help.

Sucking In

The following week I reflected upon the two spirits I had seen burning. I was still struggling with the connectivity of the burning tree of my daughter's spirit and the dragon of my mother's spirit. This morning I considered a possible connection between the close-up vision of the dragon's head and the close-up vision of Shelly's skeletal jaws. Was my mother's lack of real independence lurking around my daughter's tree to prevent her from finding her own independence? Did that tree stump "suck" my daughter into its grips? It is still all too muddled and confusing.

"Gwenn, I need your intuitive input," my voice said this morning over the phone line. I explained the 'sucking sensation' that I had seen in relation to the third spirit.

A few words of discussion were volleyed back and forth before I received any input from her. "What I get from what you've said is an unquenchable thirst. You will have to figure out what it's thirsty for. I get the feeling it is something evil, though."

"I think all of the spirits I'm trying to identify are evil," I said.

"What about relating it to life?" she continued.

"Oh? How?" I asked.

"Say someone is really craving life. They are really thirsty for living every bit of life and not wanting to miss any part of it. They are working so hard at having a life."

"That's Sue. She is working very hard at having a life. It's been a fight for her for a very long time."

"That's true," reflected Gwenn. "That third spirit may have something to do with Sue. We just have to better define it."

I knew we were both groping at this point.

I thought to myself, maybe Sue's fight for "independence" is from that evil spirit that is sucking her in. It still isn't settling right with me. That third spirit still needs to be better defined. "Love," "protect," "virtue," and now "sucking in" have all presented themselves in some form or other, but none represent the one word I'm looking for, the one that will represent the evil I feel is there.

CHAPTER THIRTY

Young Joe from the Dance

Occasionally when I meet people and tell them that I am the author of psychic phenomena books, they are most interested in my doing a psychic reading for them. I don't provide professional readings or feel that I can always see into the future, but I tell them that I will certainly make an attempt to find out whatever I can for them. I then do make a concerted effort; however, I don't believe that it is my purpose to provide this information other than through my writings.

What I get is not always understood by me and I seldom see a usefulness; however, whatever comes forth is very personal and left to the individual to decipher.

All I knew about Joe was that he was a nice young man in his early forties who liked to stay active at the dances. He is generally accompanied by a brother and a friend.

Since I have known him, he has had a girlfriend, probably older than he and of whom he is very fond. This relationship has gone on for several years; however, he tells me there is no likelihood of a permanent relationship for them. She had made herself clear about this to him.

I have also learned that Joe does not have a car and does not drive. The reasons for his not driving are kept private. He does not wish to discuss them. That means that his girlfriend must make the effort to do the commuting to pick him up, and she lives a good distance from him. Whatever his dark secrets are, they must be too painful to release, as he has never felt comfortable talking about them.

Last night I learned that he now has a job. I had not known he did not have one. I asked him what kind of work he was doing, and he said he was a "stock boy" and at a place just across the street from where he lived. I can't imagine what it is that has taken this nice young man in his forties so far from a normal life, and I do wish him well.

For Joe, the moment I meditated on his being, I saw the Blessed Mother kneeling at his side, much the same as you would see her looking over Jesus. Next, within my face, I began to feel contortions of movement, variations of pressure in different areas of the face, and a feeling of pliable configurations and rhythmical movement. I felt a strong sensation of blood pumping or pulsating going on in my head.

I presumed this was from somewhere in his past, and was in regard to whatever had happened to him. I feel he may have been involved in a life-threatening situation or may have suffered a closed-head injury. The thought crossed my mind that he may have even killed someone in a car accident. I wasn't sure if it affected his psyche or mental capability based on what I knew about him.

I then asked what was going to happen for him, what his near future held. All I saw were darkened shadows with muted light backgrounds. I would have liked to have seen more brightness in his future.

CHAPTER THIRTY-ONE

In Sync

My friend, Kristen, and I were meeting in the downtown area of Mt. Carmel, a city between our two homes. We were going to take in an evening of mixing with friends, hearing one of the concerts performed on the riverfront, and seeing the fireworks display for the pre-Fourth of July and season kickoff. This was a very popular event which brought city dwellers from surrounding areas many miles away.

Our original plan was to meet at a restaurant parking lot and take one car into town because traffic would be heavy and parking limited. The restaurant was located on my side of the destination city. Kristen was ready before I was and called when leaving her house. While driving, she found traffic so heavy that she called from her cell phone to say it would be difficult to get to our scheduled meeting place. We then decided to take both cars into the town and meet at a particular restaurant where music was being played in an outside patio area.

Just as I hung up the phone from talking with her and had said I was walking out the door, I turned and knocked a bottle of nail polish from the counter onto the floor. The bottle shattered into many pieces getting nail polish all over the kitchen cabinets, floor tile, and into the tile grout. Of course, I had to clean that up before leaving the house. I considered calling her right back but decided that with so much traffic in town it wouldn't matter if I was a few minutes late.

While driving, Kristen noticed some odor had become prevalent in her car. She had difficulty determining what it was that she could smell. It was clearly not something from the car. It was not a car component and not the smell of gasoline fumes or diesel fuel. She surmised it smelled like nail polish, but that didn't make any sense to her at all. She dismissed her thought.

When me met, I told her what had happened. The evening progressed, and toward the end, when we were alone again, she explained of the smell of nail polish she had encountered in her car while driving. She was not as spiritual as I, but knew I would understand and appreciate the occurrence.

My reply was, "Are we in sync, or what? I guess I didn't need to call you to tell you what happened."

Other similar things have happened concerning odor or fragrance. I was busily doing many things at once as I often did. I was trying to complete all of the many self-assigned tasks in getting work done on my writing and marketing on the Web.

The TV was on, as I was trying to catch the weather report for an outdoor graduation party I was going to attend. As I passed through the hallway from my home office and through the living room to the kitchen, I could smell the strong fragrance of Gardenias. When I looked up at the television, there were Gardenias on the screen.

"What do you suppose that message was all about?" I said to Gwenn.

At the same time, we both said, "Stop and smell the flowers!"

I have another friend whom I have met over the Internet in marketing one of my books who tells me this story:

> My daughter was killed a few years ago on July 18. She always wore a musk perfume. I'm a single man, now, and have never dated a lady that wore musk perfume. Every once in a while, when I'm at home, I can smell that musk perfume. I know she is here with me. She is one of my Guardian Angels, and some day I would like to learn how to contact her.

CHAPTER THIRTY-TWO

In Due Time

Both of my children were experiencing relatively happy times in their lives. Certainly, not everything was perfect, but it was far better for each of them than it had been for many years.

Sue was the happiest she had been since her first marriage now that she and Norm bought a high-rise condominium and moved in together. She did not like her current job, but now was confident enough in herself that she could put up with the mismanagement because she knew she didn't have to. It was a great stride in maturity for her.

I might also add that Sue's disposition has never been better. I dare say she tolerates Norm's pattern of taking out the elements of his dissatisfaction on the ones he loves, but she has not been this happy for a long, long time. They have lived together for more than a year now, and I'd say they are very content together. Sue finally got what she wanted and is no longer frustrated.

Doug, now rid of a dying business that he and his father both ran, was free to find a new career for himself and continue his college education. He was not without the recent aftermath of the lost business: an exorbitant debt had been levied by the state for unpaid taxes, and an unsettled bill with the IRS for same. The debt was supposedly caused by newly purchased malfunctioning equipment, thus creating the need for a lawsuit against the manufacturer. The purpose of a prospective lawsuit would hopefully offset some of this business debt.

According to business statute, I believe the suit could not be started until there was proof of debt; therefore, with tax debts solidified, it was the right time to begin such an endeavor.

Doug asked for my recommendation of an attorney, since he knew I had dated a couple and had become friends with another whom I had hired for my own cause. I normally lived a much simpler life, without these complexities, but did have need to hire one.

Doug certainly had his own repertoire of attorneys after being in business with his father, but a new one was always in order with a new pursuit. I recommended Steve, as I felt it might be his area of expertise. I also knew, being informed by my attorney friend, Bud Wiseman, that Steve had recently won a wonderful case worth a lot of money.

I had not had any contact with Steve for about four years now, but he had never left my thoughts or my heart. I knew he was a soul mate from many years past, and had accepted that our short dating encounter was all we were to share in this lifetime. Nevertheless, my watchful eye always looked for him in likely places we had frequented, and I continually looked for his home on the lake to go up for sale in a local waterfront brokers circular.

I perused that circular each time it arrived, but thankfully did not see Steve's house listed. That meant to me that his life had not changed from what I knew it to be. He was probably still dating the same girl he met during our supposed intermission and I assumed had dated her ever since. I had been told by Lillian, our mutual friend, that he was quite serious about her but did not want to re-marry. After the initial pain of that information, I was satisfied in knowing what I had learned.

Doug contacted Steve about this potential case, and Steve was interested. They met one afternoon at Steve's office, and Doug was to gather more information for him and they would meet again. Doug was coming over to do some electrical work for me on my sprinkling system the day he met with Steve.

"How did your meeting go with Steve," I asked.

"Oh, fine," Doug replied. "He asked how you were doing."

I relished in the thoughts that followed.

"He's interested in the case, and I'm to gather some more information before I see him again."

"Oh, that's good." I wondered if Steve might be taking the case because of me. No, I decided, that was not the reason. He would not compromise himself to a loss if he did not feel the case had merit.

"How did you meet him, anyway?" asked Doug.

"At a dance for single people," I said.

"Oh. He's married, isn't he?" queried Doug.

"I don't know. He might be by now."

"Well he must be. I called his house, and a woman answered and said it was his wife."

The sting pained my heart again, but I knew it was okay. I didn't want Doug to know how I felt inside. I'm not sure anyone but Gwenn understood the depth of my feelings for Steve, and more importantly why. A six-month dating relationship of over four years ago was not a logical reason for feelings lasting this long. It was only because Steve was a very deep love from some lifetime or lifetimes ago, and I had recognized him as such.

Steve, I knew, saw the love between us from the start, but he did not recognize or understand the basis for his feelings. He fantasized of a permanent relationship between us and often acknowledged the attraction he felt for me.

He was interested in the subject of reincarnation, but I knew had not taken the time to delve into such a topic. He wanted to be the interpreter of the visions I received, but I knew no one could replace Gwenn's talent.

When Steve asked if I could see any visual image in regard to him, I reported that I could. What I saw was the likeness to the famous Mt. Rushmore stone carvings in South Dakota of four United States' presidents (George Washington, Abraham Lincoln, Theodore Roosevelt, and Thomas Jefferson).

What I had seen in regard to Steve were six carvings. Four were male and two were female. I supposed that two of the males were Steve and his late father, for whom he had great admiration, and the other two males were his devoted sons. The two women were his mother and his current wife, who were clearly bickering. I might surmise that they were all very hard, inflexible personalities of great importance to Steve. His divorce was not finalized at that time.

I had fully prepared myself for just such information to come to me in regard to Steve, but it still hurt. Brenda had predicted I would learn of such information when she was at my house much earlier this year.

When I knew that Doug was going to call Steve, I recalled this information that had been imprinted in my mind. I made a point to tell my closest of friends, Gwenn, Mary and Kristen, that Doug was going to be calling Steve, and I would probably find out that he was either engaged or married.

Gwenn understood my relationship with Steve began eons ago--perhaps a thousand years or more--and the feelings I still had and why.

My quick analysis told me that after Steve won that notable case, he then had enough money to feel worthy of asking his lady friend's hand in marriage. It may have been partially to agree to her desires, as he was an honorable man, but I was sure a love existed between them. I do wish them happiness together. I understood that our lives were not meant to meld anymore this lifetime than they already had.

It couldn't have been more than a week later that the circular of waterfront homes again arrived at my house. As usual, I was going to peruse its fold-out contents, but didn't have to. Steve's house was the first one featured on the front page. I recognized the street name, then the picture, and finalized it by verifying the street address against my personal home address book. Steve's home was for sale.

I knew the house would appear for sale in that specific circular, but I wasn't to find out until I had received the information that he was now married. I could now let him go.

Gwenn refers back to the concept that "time" is only something that man learned to place on elements of this lifetime, and that really all things were happening at once. That is why I knew Steve's house would be for sale and appear in that circular.

The best description I have found for my understanding of this concept of time is this: all of life is happening at once. What we see is a snapshot view of each segment. On earth, we see these snapshots as a time series. Each one is presented as "this is now," thus we feel the passing of time.

CHAPTER THIRTY-THREE

March Reading

The time is now approaching Winter, and I thought about the Tarot card reading I had by Brenda in March. I reviewed what she had told me now for any relevance to my life this past year. This is what she said.

You will be getting answers to family questions.

I feel these answers might be in regard to the untamed family spirits in my life.

You will be getting money from new sources, two large amounts from your own efforts, maybe in the summer months.

Unfortunately, the receipt of this money was not in regard to my work efforts or winning the lottery. First I borrowed a large sum of money to build an addition on my home. Next, I refinanced my home to cover both my current mortgage and the new loan.

Recognition will be coming to me for something I have done, something I have created.

Yes, I'd like to think it was for my first book, 'Visual Encounters.'

There will be a painful decision-making, a separation of something. It is important for you and your sanity. It will need a yes or no answer, and I feel the answer should be yes to keep your sanity. I see you carrying something out.

Yes, it was a painful decision-making process. I had to separate myself from an income-producing environment in order to complete writing a movie script and continue marketing my current book.

I agonized over turning away work when I needed the money, and never intended to refinance in order to incorporate the loan for the addition. I had planned to return to work and pay off the loan.

The question may have been, "Shall I continue to finish my on-going tasks and not return to work at this time?" The answer was "Yes!" and it was a matter of keeping my sanity. Had I gone back to work, the inability to continue marketing of my book would have left me terribly bereft. It was something I was being driven to do. I definitely felt I needed to carry this assignment out to completion.

I will be doing some travel with purpose. I need to experience something, find out information; there is some information that I will discover. I will have fun on my travel, but will also find out information. This information will help me in omitting negativity. Once pinpointed, there will be latent gifts flying out of me.

About one month ago I decided to give my British friend, Duncan, a telephone call. My purpose was to ask him if he planned to travel to England the following year. My need was to research information that has obsessed me for several years. Namely, it is the tombstones that I saw in my vivid vision as well as old, cinderblock buildings that haunt me. Answers in regard to these tombstones and other past-life matters is what I seek.

I have searched the grounds of many graveyards for tombstones that resemble those in my vision. They are not here. All of the head stones I have found in the United States are not the right size, shape or depth, not even in the very old sections. The closest I can find are from the 1800's. I have watched movies from many lands, and a glimpse of a graveyard in England tells me I might find them there. I also feel a deep need to see England's old cities and buildings that are hundreds of years old. A channeler told me that my cinderblock building is in England. A trip is planned with Duncan for 2001.

Look for an announcement, a social gathering and gossip—all positive. The announcement is concerning a child or children; it will be concerning a Pisces. "Oh, Sue and Doug--

they're both Pisces," Brenda said. I acknowledged that they were.

No news, announcement or social gathering has taken place, except for the announcement by Doug's current live-in girlfriend. She told me that her brother's girlfriend is pregnant and they will have a child. There is no plan for them to marry at this time, but their relationship is fine.

There is a new love entering your life. I feel it will be someone that you don't know. There will be someone else entering your life. You will look at this person and will have the feeling that you know them. It will be someone from a past life.

No new love has entered my life except for a couple of brief infatuations. The charm of meeting the first gentleman wore off quickly as he was unreliable. The enchantment of the second never developed although I feel it could have been captivating for a time.

I consulted the Tarot immediately upon meeting him. I was told there would be no long-term relationship as he had suggested. I was also told that he had a decision to make in regard to a current situation. I suspected that he was not free and he has only called once since our meeting.

The person who entered my life that I

definitely recognized was my plumber's assistant for the new addition on my home. The first two times he appeared on the job, I questioned him extensively to find out from where I might know him. There has been no connection that we can make, and I was not the least bit familiar to him. However, I felt that I recognized and knew him immediately.

Taking information from a few psychic sources, this person is to give me an indication of something important that happened in the past life with the cinderblock building that haunts me. I feel he was the doctor's aide in a past life where I was a nurse.

Some revelations will be coming in my life, and if I had found out earlier, I wouldn't have wanted to know them. I will be glad I know them now and can rid myself of 'negativities.'

I most definitely knew when the opportunity presented itself that I would learn that Steve was engaged or married. At the point that I was to be given this information, it was okay for me to know. I could accept it with much lesser pain than I had experienced in the past.

I just learned of another engagement of one of my male friends for whom I have felt a real attachment, and that information, too, has come at a time that is quite acceptable to me.

To use Brenda's term, the only 'negativities' I

can imagine is that probably neither of them would have been right for me.

In areas of conflict, I will win. Don't back away from a good fight. My real 'clair-audio' will take over and I will have the ability to hear without physical ears.

I did have the opportunity to work a great job for a good company this Fall. The assignment probably would have lasted much longer than it did, except for my non-acceptance of the constant ridicule by a perfectionist boss. When the time and circumstances were right, I told him just how I felt. I'm sure he did not know how to handle my contempt for his overly meticulous ways. He released me from the assignment immediately.

I have never before been so adamant in releasing my feelings and anger. I did not back down; in fact, I gave him little room for comment. Something just took over, and I was soon released from further burden of him. In essence, I believe I won.

I'd say that my reading and analysis of the prevailing circumstances of my life this past year are pretty accurate. I feel it is good to review these projections.

CHAPTER THIRTY-THREE

Ribbon Candy

Aunt Addie has now passed on, and through her funeral, I was again put in touch with out-of-state relatives that I hadn't seen for years. I also met one of my cousin's daughters for the first time. She was a delightful, warm and friendly young woman. With accessibility through the Internet today, I have now established contact with both my cousin in Florida and his daughter in Texas.

Loraine had now read portions of my book, "Visual Encounters," and had found that I receive these strange-but-true symbolic readings of people. She asked me, through an Internet e-mail, if I had ever received a vision of her dad.

I told her "No," but the next day I saw a mental picture and sent an e-mail back with only the words "Ribbon Candy."

She did not catch on to that being a response to her question. I then had to reiterate her question and my full answer.

I then passed the information on to her dad.

"Your daughter, Loraine, asked if I had seen a vision of you. I replied that I had not. As usual, a delayed reaction occurs and I saw 'ribbon candy' in my mind's eye."

The rest follows: Of course, I had to "inquire" with my counterpart for further input.

Gwenn's response was this:

> My first response to "ribbon candy" was a sweet guy with multiple interests or personalities who is coming and going but not making much progress.

I replied: On the ribbon candy, I think you're pretty close. He is a really sweet guy, and with your insight, I would agree his life has had many paths and has had its share of ups and downs (like the candy).

In summation, I forwarded this information to my cousin:

> A very sweet and colorful person whose life has multi-paths and interests, and moderate-to-extraordinary ups and downs.

You're free to comment!

I did not receive a response. That concerned me, so I wrote again asking if I had offended him. His response was this:

> Believe me, there was no offense. Thought the vision quite interesting and much on the mark.
>
> Sorry for the delay in answering but things have been quite hectic at the office lately.

On July 5th they brought in an Assistant Controller. It came as quite a surprise to me. My boss and I go all the way back to Korea and he didn't even give me a 'heads up.' One of the Assistant Controller's first assignments was to learn the payroll processing (something I have been doing for the past 10-1/2 years) as quickly as possible, the excuse being that we have been too long without a payroll back-up.

Funny, there has been no urgency to train a back-up for payroll for the past 10-1/2 years. In addition to that, the Credit and Collection Manager has found favor with the powers to be and is beginning to involve herself with a few of my accounts.

Is this beginning to paint a picture? Will attempt to get some straight answers from my boss today. Don't believe this is possible but I will try.

Obviously, he was about to experience another extraordinary situation. The week that followed was news that he was going to be through by October of this year. It would be a "voluntary" retirement—imagine that! Now his plans are to sell his current home, and return to Texas to live near his children.

I was only too familiar with this type of treatment, as I had been placed in a situation that forced me out of a Corporation to which I had given many faithful years.

CHAPTER THIRTY-FOUR

More Family Connectivity

Now I was also e-mailing Eleanor, the wife of this cousin's brother, more frequently. Funerals always seem to bring families closer together.

She and I normally sent only selected and appropriate jokes received on to each other, and when I was forwarding one, the thought occurred to me that I should ask how her husband, Bill, was doing.

Bill had also been retired out early but had a medical problem as well. He had a severe back injury from years past, and his work required heavy lifting. While he got by for many years, he was later involved in a car accident that put his back out of whack permanently. He now was unable to do many things he enjoyed including his lifetime hobby of gardening.

As I wrote to Eleanor, I had a strong feeling about my cousin and was about to ask, "How's Bill doing?" I refrained, chastising myself by thinking, "If you really want to know, call!" But I didn't.

The next day I received an e-mail from Loraine in Texas who said her Uncle Bill was in the hospital. Then I called Eleanor!

When she asked how I found out Bill was in the hospital, I told her: "This is very strange, and not.

Yesterday I sent you an e-mail and almost asked how Bill was doing. I had a strong feeling I should ask, but didn't. I had planned to call. Then I got an e-mail from Loraine who said her Uncle Bill was in the hospital. I didn't really 'listen' to the voice in my head. Shame on me!"

CHAPTER THIRTY-FIVE

Soul Mates

My on-earth guide, Gwenn, was always looking out for me. She called to tell me some information she had received through reading that she felt she should pass on. Many times, information that she learned she felt was for the purpose of helping other people. This was the message she felt necessary to pass on to me.

> I re-read a section of the book I just finished, referring to the men in the author's life. It hits a chord with your life, especially with Steve and Mike who were placed in your life with a purpose.
>
> Basically she was reviewing her relationships with the men in her life and identified that they were all 'soul' connections. It was not who they were in this lifetime that was important, but that she recognized them at a soul level. She recognized that their time together in this life was for a definite purpose.
>
> She determined that when each relationship hit a certain point, and their existence together satisfied a purpose, it would then fall apart.
>
> Some time in the future you may want to read this book, or at least parts of it, to get more understanding of the men you have encountered 'with purpose' in your life.

"Thanks," I said. "I'll have to read it some time."

I never felt closer to a soul mate from a past life than I have about Steve. I'm sure we had a wonderful "love" one or more times in our many lives together. I think our part together in this life was to ease us both through a time of transition.

Then, with Mike, there was no question in either of our minds that we were literally thrown together with a "mad-for-each-other" love—but only for a time. Then it became time to separate. While I cannot relate to having known him in a specific former life, we experienced an immediate comfort with one another and our time together was definitely with purpose.

The second revelation I learned this year was in reference to Frank-O and his recent engagement. In regard to our relationship, I haven't found the answer to that puzzle yet. He was a gentleman who clearly didn't match my ultimate needs. However, he was someone who was always very important to me and I just as important to him. The importance had to do with feelings of an intimate nature; however, we were not ever drawn to be together.

His form of attraction to me mirrors the element of importance as well. I often hear from his lady friends how he constantly talks about me, yet our actual time together has been minimal. Similarly, I am just as apt to find myself talking about him to my friends.

Our friendship dates back several years, but a relationship was never consummated. There is no doubt that it ever will be; however, a form of love exists without foundation that cannot be denied.

I remember reading a book about two other soul mates that found each other both as males in this lifetime, but recognized that they had been male and female lovers in the past. They now were of inappropriate gender and age to have a coupled relationship, with one in his late forties and the other a young man in his early twenties. Recognizing each other now and feeling some profound love of the past gave way to a warm embrace of one another to share this known felt emotion.

Reading all this gives me some inclination that Frank-O and I were "something" together, related by blood perhaps or as lovers at one or more times. However, reading about the endearing embrace of two males made me feel very uncomfortable.

CHAPTER THIRTY-SIX

Sorting Through the Mysteries

Never are all questions answered or all things defined, as much as we would like them to be. One can only recapture the things of importance and try to make sense out of all of the pieces. The spiritual world, of course, always leaves holes in logic and nothing is for certain. Some things are left to your own understanding, acceptance and beliefs.

I feel, however, that I have now come upon an explanation for the last of the three family spirits and have come to understand the evil connotation of the dragon for which I so desperately searched. My assessment even amazes me.

I had gone to see a movie about death row in a prison. It featured lead rolls of a soft-hearted prison guard and an inmate who had supernatural powers. It was an exceptional movie, and of course, one in which I had a keen interest due to its spiritual value.

I later read the reviews searching for others' evaluations of the spiritual implications. I found little other than that the inmate seemed to possess a tremendous, supernatural gift of healing and of raising the dead. I also found a biblical reference to the healings of God in 1 Corinthians 12 and the necessity for both the healer and subject to be deeply committed to the healings of God in order to achieve a successful treatment.

At first, the movie made no impact on me except for it being a pretty entertaining flick. Months later, after talking about it with one of my friends, a very clear understanding came to mind putting all of the pieces of my mysterious puzzle together.

Of course, it had a catalyst to start this understanding process. I had been perusing catalogs one day, and as a matter of practice, always tore out pictures of things that represented some proximity to my psychic mental visions. This time the dragon that represented my mother's spirit was a *gargoyle*.

When I first described the dragon, I spoke of the "cutting words of the tongue." Aside from that, I didn't find this dragon particularly harmful. I read up on dragons and found that they had protective qualities, and were sometimes thought to be a thing of beauty.

In researching chronicles of the dragon, I found that throughout European history, it was often a symbol of monstrous power and danger. A dragon was also known as a demon or of having demonic qualities. In China it was regarded as a helpful beast and sometimes as a lucky or protective creature. In ancient times it was even the symbol of a supreme ruler or the guardian of extraordinary treasure.

My former friend, Matt, had explained that gargoyles were thought to keep the "evil spirits away." I had known nothing about them previously. I always thought they were just grotesque figures or sculptures.

It was all coming clear to me now. In the movie, the kind-hearted guard and others who worked the prison's death row had taken the gifted inmate to their friend's house to heal his ill wife who was suffering from an untreatable tumor.

In the incidents shown, the inmate was able to 'suck' or withdraw the evil spirits from a person's body that were causing the ailment and then disperse them into the air to disintegrate. In the case of the ill wife, he purposely held the withdrawn evil in, temporarily making himself ill. He later dispersed the elements directly into the soul he believed was evil and deserving of the treatment.

The picture of the dragon gargoyle put all things into perspective for me. All of the words I had been given seemingly by chance either psychically or spiritually all began to fit perfectly. The words "love," "to protect," "a sucking in," and "virtue" all played back in my mind, and the mystery was finally to be solved.

My mother's spirit was a dragon gargoyle, put there to protect me from evil. Through her love for me, she knowingly held in the evil spirits that I would have otherwise encountered. She made herself seem evil at times while keeping as much of the evil from me as she could—certainly a virtuous quality. It is those restless, evil spirits from which I was protected that my mission is now to resolve.

All of those years, she had kept the demons at bay, and held them within so that I would not be harmed. She put her own relationship with me at risk in order to protect me.

When the dragon burned, along with the jagged tree stump, she could no longer hold the demons in. They were divulged and disgorged at this point into the open air to disintegrate and exist no longer.

Does that mean that the evil spirits pertaining to "power" and "independence" have now fully been dealt with? In my estimation my cousin has certainly conquered her mission to find independence. This appears to be an untamed spirit in her family lineage from her father's side, although I cannot say it has not crossed over to my immediate family. I seemed to have been born with it, but my children have had to achieve independence in their lives.

The "power" in the family lineage, I now believe stopped with me. It was my lesson to learn. It has now been formerly addressed. I rightfully acknowledge that it is a quality that can be used and misused. While I firmly believe in the power of the mind and of healing, I also accept and respect the cautionary rules of its use.

While I've learned that its use can be overpowering and destroy meaningful relationships, it can also be used appropriately to accomplish virtuous tasks. In regard to relationships, I was recently told through a channeler that my Spirit Guide had recognized that I lost a true love. I felt that his comments were in regard to Matt. I was told he would be there to watch over me and to see that this didn't happen again. He felt that I kept myself too protected, and that I needed to let myself go and to feel life.

Whereas I had thought that my daughter and I were part of the long line of family members dealing with the same spirit of "power," I find that she had one of her own to address. She was to learn "responsibility" which was a seemingly difficult task. Although she may have more lessons to learn, she now has attained "responsibility" to an admirable level. It is a level that even she has not yet recognized.

I haven't decided if the confines of the tree stump were there to keep my daughter from progressing or to protect her from an evil that surrounded it. Perhaps my mother's "power" was strong enough to protect us both. That may remain an unknown, but since both spirits died together, I suspect this may be true. May the demons that perpetuated the lessons of "independence," "power" and "responsibility" forever rest in peace and may I be able to carry out the implausible virtues of love and protection as shown by my mother.